COME SLEEP WITH ME

For Joyce
I hope you enjoy reading
about some of my adventures!
with love and laughter

Stephanie

COME SLEEP WITH ME

STEPHANIE HILL

The Book Guild Ltd

First published in Great Britain in 2019 by
The Book Guild Ltd
9 Priory Business Park
Wistow Road, Kibworth
Leicestershire, LE8 0RX
Freephone: 0800 999 2982
www.bookguild.co.uk
Email: info@bookguild.co.uk
Twitter: @bookguild

Typeset in 11pt Adobe Garamond Pro

Printed and bound by CPI Group (UK) Ltd, Croydon, CR0 4YY

ISBN 978 1912881 178

British Library Cataloguing in Publication Data.
A catalogue record for this book is available from the British Library.

For my beautiful, bonkers, brilliant parents…
Thanks for loving me whatever I do and wherever I go

And to the rest of my family both those by birth
and those by choice….

THANKYOU…heaps and oodles!!

We have laughed with abandon, loved unconditionally, hugged
fantastically and skipped and played and danced and sung.
You have let me cry to get stronger, let me escape for adventure
and let me know that I am loved…
the MOST precious feeling in the world

My life is an amazing journey made so perfect
by all of you gorgeous people
You know who you are and you all know that I think
you're brilliant… you make my heart sing

Oh, and to those who said I couldn't, shouldn't,
mustn't and won't…
Thank you… for the inspiration!

And Remember:
Laughter is the shortest distance between two people

CONTENTS

INTRODUCTION

People to Sleep With Me

It's funny how people earn a living, isn't it? After many years living overseas on the idyllic island of Bermuda I was back in the UK and very keen for people to pay me money to sleep with me in my own home. I wasn't concerned about their age, their race or their religious affiliations. Heck, I wasn't even concerned about their gender. What I was concerned about was getting people into bed.

They could be friends spending quality time together, families travelling in a group or couples looking for a romantic interlude. I didn't mind. I was desperate and I had bills to pay so as long as they had the money to pay up front and not do anything too abhorrent then I was willing to have them. And frankly I wasn't in a position to care whether they respected me in the morning… it would be nice if they did but it certainly wasn't going to be a prerequisite.

It was clear that there were many people who offered services which might be similar to mine but I intended to go over and above the average and offer them a grand breakfast, a few kind words and a large cuppa after having slept with me. Who could say fairer than that!?

1

If they wanted anonymity they could park up at the back of the house and come in through the side door under cover of night and leave early in the morning, unseen by neighbours or passing strangers. Or if they chose they could come to the front door in broad daylight, be greeted eagerly by me and swept upstairs in a matter of minutes. I didn't mind as long as they stayed.

I had decided to be in the business of having people sleep with me for money and I knew it was going to be tough. I didn't know how tough. People have all sorts of weird and wonderful requests and want all sorts of different things in the bedroom. It was up to me to try and accommodate them so they would recommend me to their friends and family.

Luckily I had a partner at the time who was very open-minded about the whole process. He understood the need to have multiple and various visitors to my bed. He encouraged it actually and even occasionally discussed ways in which I could persuade more people to come and languish in my sheets.

We discussed what to do if they were a couple or single or foreign or elderly and how best to attract people from different parts of the world.

At this point I feel I should make myself clear. And for those of you who may have gone off at a tangent in the wrong direction, I am not offering *me* as part of the service in the sheets.

Please come back from the brink of your thought pattern and understand that I am in fact talking about entering the land of bed and breakfast ownership and my desire for people to come stay in my beds was completely above board. (Which, did you know, was originally a gambling term referring to the fact that a gambler whose hands were above the board or gaming table could not engage in trickery such as changing cards.)

I bought a beautiful big house with many rooms, all of which needed to be inhabited by paying guests in order for me to stay in business and pay the mortgage. I had once worked for Trusthouse

Forte as a manager, had done some waitressing jobs and knew how to clean a bathroom, but frankly that is where my hospitality business acumen ended. When I started out I had no idea of how I was going to get lots of people to come and stay with me. I knew a bit about marketing, firmly believed in the power of networking but knew neither the area I moved to nor the different avenues or publications in which to advertise. Instead, I did what I have done many times before and I took a punt! I bought a business that was ailing, in a house that needed lots of work, in a place I knew no one and I decided to make it successful. The pages hereafter contain some thoughts, some guests and some strange occurrences. But mainly they contain me, my ramblings and some of my adventures in B&B land and beyond.

*

This book started off as a blog many years ago for a friend's online magazine. I called it *Beds and a Bit o' Brekky* then because that's what I thought my life would be. I had no idea of the wealth of people, the breadth of experience or the wholehearted success this part of my life would be.

It has been fabulous.

But here is the thing. If you are hoping for a book that teaches you the best practices to run a successful bed and breakfast, look elsewhere. If you are looking for a tacky book revealing nasty secrets about guests then think again. If you want a travelogue of epic proportions akin to Patrick Leigh Fermor's *A Time of Gifts* then this book isn't for you. However, if you are interested in a journey through life loosely based around a B&B in the UK with a few anecdotes about my travelling life and some of the intriguing people I have met, then I hope you enjoy my meanderings!

I have learnt so very much from my years as a landlady. I have learnt about compassion, about communication and about consideration for others and I have seen first hand how people can be genuinely connected to each other in a way that makes your heart soar.

I have an absolute unshakeable belief in the power of humanity and that life is about kindness, curiosity and potential and when you amalgamate those together you can create a rich and wondrous life. Kindness connects us, potential helps us evolve and positivity will always eclipse the negative.

I would like to say that all the places and people in this book are fictitious… they aren't! I would like to say that it's all come from my amazing imagination… it hasn't. It's come from years of enjoying life in B&B land and the world beyond… enjoy!

CHAPTER 1

The Unexpected

It simply never occurred to me that I would one day be standing outside my own B&B with a flowery pinny on, wiping my dishwashing soapy hands after waving guests off and saying to myself, 'My goodness, my bollards need painting!!!'

I also never thought I would one day be here recalling tales of heartache and happiness along with stories that continually remind me of the kindness and generosity of spirit that is key to our humanity.

I find myself eager to share experiences about how we moved in and met our first guests. How we were like mad Labrador puppies full of eager excitement and how our forays into the world of the cash and carry filled us with dread at spending what appeared to be the national debt.

I want to tell you about how we endured power cuts, floods, broken toilets, strange requests and things that really did go bump in the night. There have been bizarre guests who will never be named, but who will live in my memory forever, and there have been legendary guests who will live in my heart forever. We have enjoyed a village that is vibrant and alive and quirky and mad and we have grown to love friends as the business has grown. And during all the escapades, endurances and craziness, what consistently amazes and brings me great joy is the sheer loveliness of people.

We can all listen to the media prattle on about the downsides of things and how we are becoming estranged and alienated from each other. We can listen to reports about how no one communicates anymore.

Well, I have to disagree!

When you get people round a table eating breakfast, there are few barriers and people actually talk to one another. What might start off as a quick conversation about where to get the tour bus in Bath gets extended to work-related conversations, then to cultural exchanges and usually a giggle or two! Many times it has become even better and people arrange to meet up in Bath, to share transport or perhaps have a pint in the local pub when they return from their day's excursions.

These impromptu gatherings which usually extend into the wee hours are the source of great amusement at the time and equal hilarity when the guests come to breakfast, only then realising that whilst I had been partying with them till 2am, I had then got up at six to create their breakfast experience!

I never thought I would get attached to inanimate objects like a house… or bollards but that's what happens in life isn't it? The unexpected!

My concern for the paint on my bollards are not the words of the girl from the Midlands with a wanderlust who, at seventeen, had taken off on travels that would lead her to many continents and a variety of cultures and which had brought her back to the UK on a whim after a chance meeting with a lovely man called Miles! I had been to the USA and down through Mexico, spent heaps of time in South East Asia and loved Australasia. India had come as a complete surprise, as had Russia and the more unexplored areas of Europe.

Not these words for a girl who a) doesn't like to cook, b) can't cook, c) thinks domesticity is an interruption to her social life and for whom the epitome of routine is cleaning her teeth in the morning!

How on earth did I get here? Do you ever ask yourself the same question?

I know I was born to be around people and have always loved helping people feel a bit more jolly and a little bit better by a kind word or deed, or by simply laughing at or with me.

I was born to investigate and enquire and engage and discover.

I had always loved exploring and finding out different places to visit. School reports said I had an enquiring mind... Mum said I was nosey!

But I had travelled a lot, so finding myself having the bollard conversation in my head was a little disconcerting.

I guess my desire to engage and meet new people urged me into B&B land. It was based partly in wanting to repay some of the wonderful kindnesses that I had been shown in the past whilst wandering the globe, prior to entering the world of B&B.

*

In the previous twenty years I had travelled many times to the United States of America and crossed it from coast to coast three different ways. One of these included a trip via a great company called AA Driveaway who are based in Boston. They offered the opportunity for me to deliver vehicles from one destination to another, giving me a maximum of seven days to complete the journey. I intended to go from the East to the West Coast of the USA. There are a lot of miles you can do in seven days and a variety of detours (which of course were logged with the company). I had a fabulous time! The first collection from Boston was a pretty run-of-the-mill four-door blue Mazda belonging to a family who were relocating to San Antonio in Texas. They wanted to fly to their new home and have their car and other belongings delivered separately.

Hence the need for me to drive their car all that way. So, after clearing the hiring process with passport details and driving licence number it was off out onto the open road! Now there are a variety of routes I could have taken, but I wanted to see things like the world's biggest ball of twine, Buffalo Bill's resting place and the Painted Desert, but they were a long way off. Instead I opted for an Atlantic City gambling den, the Liberty Bell of the USA as well as enjoying the craziness of Tallahassee and the jazz culture of New Orleans. I headed south then west… ish!

And so it was that I hopped on Interstate Highway 95 and, bypassing the outskirts of that great metropolis New York, I travelled south detouring to the den of iniquity that is Atlantic City! I only had to be in this massive neon centre for twelve hours or so before I realised that, although the song 'Under the Boardwalk' might recollect times of gentleness and the fun of the 1960s, this simply wasn't what one encounters now.

Gambling is the main reason people venture here and once I had squandered my ten-dollar wager and seen people huddled hopelessly over a penny slot machine drowning in a sea of cigarette smoke and disappointment, I was off onto the highway once more. I know there must be other parts of Atlantic City that are lovely but this young cat wasn't waiting to see!

Philadelphia is home to the famous Liberty Bell of Independence and it felt right to stop in and see this symbol of freedom, as it did to pop into Williamsburg and understand some colonial history. The interstates in the USA, as you will probably know, are huge! They are wide and long and well kept in many places, and the signs hover above you with fascinating names like Roanoke Rapids, Elmira Crossroads and a quaint little place called Rosebud.

Savannah, Georgia conjures up all sorts of romantic notions for me. Swirling white tulle dresses, floaty hats and clandestine kisses behind parasols with mint juleps being sipped in the heat of the summer. What I had not expected, and what the guidebooks don't tell you, is how glorious it is to simply walk round the historic district of Savannah on a summer's evening with places like the Gingerbread House and the Cathedral of St John the Baptist offering amazing examples of architecture. It was quite breathtaking. They might not have been in floaty dresses, but the people of Savannah are hospitable to the max with me being offered drinks and dinner by a friendly couple who had a friend called John in London and thought I might know him!

From the relative sanity of Savannah I headed west towards my final destination of San Antonio, Texas. But there was a lot to see on the way and I was constantly bombarded with opportunities to view state parks, historical monuments and places called things like Little Bert's Big Fat Diner which, by viewing the number of double-bellied humans leaving, really lived up to its name.

I did feel the need to stop in to New Orleans, and my goodness what a treat! Olde worlde charm, live music, great food and dancing in the streets. I even ended up at a wedding as the couple had decided that, instead of a formal 'sit down' private affair, they wanted their small congregation to walk, dance, drink and eat with them through the streets of New Orleans; I happened to be there.

Cyril the groom came up to me sheepishly and asked, "Are you really from England?"

"I truly am," I replied and smiled benignly.

"Your accent is too cute, we all were listening to it and wondered if you might like to come and visit with us."

"I would be delighted to come and chat with you," I replied in what in hindsight was a very plummy British accent.

I followed him to the remaining entourage and seven hours later, after way too many tequila shots and having been stuffed with gumbo, muffelettas and jambalaya, I was told I would not stay in a motel but must enjoy some traditional Southern hospitality. I did and spent two days with these lovely people!

Finally, into the lovely city of San Antonio and, after dropping off my by now much-beloved little Mazda, affectionately known as Sid, I was able to wander the River Walk that makes this city so delightful. Bars and restaurants and chatter and boats and walkers and runners and families and lovers all enjoy this central area, whilst the Alamo offers an intriguing insight into Mexican and American history.

Due to AA Driveaway regulations I had to collect my next vehicle the next morning. So after staying several nights in different cheap motels, slightly sleazy hotels, lay-bys and hostels, I decided to have a little luxury in a so-called 3* Scottish Inns hotel. I think this is where my passion for hospitality came about. This was the worst place ever!

No lighting in the room, apart from a single hanging, grubby bulb, bedding which was torn and, to add insult to injury, the odd cockroach decided to join me for a snooze! Arrgh… never would I naïvely 'treat' myself to a pay-up-front-before-you-see-the-room 3* motel again.

I arrived by taxi at my next collection point the following morning and what greeted me just about made up for the experience of the Roach Motel! Sitting waiting to be delivered to Denver, Colorado some 900 miles away was a beautiful, shiny, black Chevrolet Corvette Convertible… I was in seventh heaven! I couldn't believe my luck.

In the office, Ursula, in a break from loudly chewing gum, asked for my details then gave me the story of the owner who had bought the car, done very few miles and was relocating to Denver.

"He didn't wanna drive so far as a consequence of him being uncomfortable in the seat," I was informed.

"You OK with taking this instead of the SUV we originally had assigned to you?"

Hummm, let me think!??? Convertible, sunshine, miles and miles of open road… nope, I didn't think that would be too big an obstacle! Thanks, Ursula.

Off I toddled and got myself all set up in 'my' new wheels and looked at the map to decide which way to travel. That's when it became clear that this drive would be through some amazing landscapes and that I only had the regulatory seven days within which to complete the journey.

Not enough time, I thought.

What to do? I thought, so I retraced my steps into the office to once again find Ursula chomping on gum.

"Ursula," I enquired with what I hoped was my most endearing voice, "is there a way that I could extend the journey by a couple of days to enjoy some more of your lovely country?"

"Nope."

"Is it possible to ask your manager?"

"Nope."

"Could I pay for the extra days?"

"Nope, nope, nope," said the nice lady.

I was deflated and about to walk out of the door when I heard, "Yes, yes," from the man reading the paper in the waiting area! It turned out that this distinguished, tall, balding gentleman was Blake, the owner of the car who had heard my desperate heartfelt pleading and in his words, "With that accent" (it comes in useful sometimes), it would be his pleasure to let me use the car for another two days. Yippeee… and with oodles of British thanks I was off!

I drove via Austin, the state capital, and through the glorious northern Texas hill country into the Texas panhandle. My obvious detour was to see New Mexico and the wonders of the pueblos, tribes and nations of the Native Americans. The border sign says you are entering the 'Land of Enchantment' and, with the rituals, craftwork and the living history all around me, I was enthralled by this part of the great USA. It is also home to the world's Largest Pistachio Nut which Nate, a local guide, assured me, "Was long true real grown like that. They just put it in some sort o' juice to preserve it". OK Nate!

Cadillac Ranch in Amarillo made an interesting stop to visit the art collection of ten Cadillacs half-buried nose-first in the ground, then onto Oklahoma where I created myself an ear-worm (song stuck in your ear) that would last for days! Finally I saw the sign that said I was entering Kansas the Land of Arrs (Land of OZ!!!) Oh to have some ruby-red slippers, I thought. I visited the little-known Negro League Baseball Museum then onto the much more famous (read highly commercialised tourist trap) OZ Museum. At OZ you can click your heels whenever you please, uttering the immortal words 'There's no place like home' and everyone around you will nod with a sympathetic, knowing smile as if you are part of an elite gang. Worrying stuff!

Into Colorado and Lookout Mountain to find Buffalo Bill's grave, the Coors Brewery Museum, and onto Echo Lake and the Rocky Mountain National Park. It was along this stretch that the incident occurred.

It's about an hour from Denver to Echo Lake and the scenery on the way is stunning. So there I am top-down, music loud, cruising along, singing my heart out and I hear a noise that unsettles me... it's a siren, it's American, it's loud and by the scene in my rear-view mirror it wants me to stop!

Pulling over I gathered my wits about me and went to get out of the car, only just remembering that I should stay in the car, not reach for anything that could be construed as a gun, and keep both hands on the wheel. This I did. The vision that approached me was like something out of a movie. Tall, lean, shades on, wearing a very distinguished-looking brimmed hat and with an impressive swagger, the officer of the law came to see me.

"Hello," I said politely. "What seems to be the problem officer?"

"Maam," he said, in a delicious American drawl, "do you know the speed limit in these parts and do you have any idea how fast you were travelling?"

Recognising a potentially troublesome situation, I did at this point indulge in a wee bit of eyelid batting and perhaps a touch of fawning. All I could think of was how cross Blake, my lovely benefactor of the Corvette, would be with a speeding fine added to his car registration. So the baby blues had to be put into full force, the eyelashes fluttered along with a little incline of the head and a heart-breaking "I don't know, officer, I was mesmerised by the beauty all around me," in what I hoped was a beguiling and slightly coquettish voice.

This was clearly not my finest moment and ludicrous in retrospect, but completely necessary at the time.

"Where are you from, maam?" asked the nice officer and after sharing my heritage a little I proceeded to bleat on about the wonders of his glorious country and how amazing it all is. The poor man couldn't have possibly given me a ticket as I swooned and tried desperately to ingratiate myself to him. So, after a little chat, he stood very upright, doffed his hat and said the immortal words, "On your way maaaaaam and have a nice day." I politely went on my way.

Denver to San Francisco was the last leg of my first journey across the USA. This had to be done in a somewhat less salubrious vehicle. It was in fact a Stanley Steamer Carpet Cleaner van! Fully equipped to wash, dry and fully valet a variety of commercial and residential properties, this large transit-size van with no side windows and barely enough room for my rucksack, needed to be transported to the West Coast. I was to drive 1,350 miles in this bright yellow contraption with its company name emblazoned down the side. It was going to be a long seven days!

I planned my trip undaunted: Stanley (as my van was obviously named) and I would travel from Denver to Salt Lake through the Painted Desert to the Grand Canyon and up along Big Sur to San Francisco. The undulating salt lakes were remarkable and flâneuring (meaning someone who is wandering the streets, not with the intent of getting somewhere, but as an observer or philosopher) through downtown Salt Lake City was eventful! Mormons are very tidy people and it seemed that the entire city wore a suit and tie.

My encounter with Mormons was swift, as the conversation went like this:

"Hi, where are you from?"

"The UK."

"How do you feel about polygamy?"

"I have no thoughts about it really."

"Would you like to come inside so we can share with you some of the teachings that bring us peace?"

"No thanks, gotta run!"

I might have been interested in the magnificent organ but felt it inappropriate to mention it. I knew all about the evils of drink and promiscuity that lay ahead on the road to Nevada. So I headed there as quickly as possible!

The Painted Desert just north of Flagstaff is utterly captivating with its hues of colours of sand. But as I reached the Grand Canyon the level of hospitality in the USA ratcheted up another notch when I met Wendell and Lorraine sitting on the canyon edge. We got talking about our travels and life in general. They were about to go up in their plane to fly below the ridge of the canyon and decided that I should go with them! Whether it was my look of wonder at the canyon, my stupid grin that I had actually made it, or that 'cute' English accent again I don't know, but next thing I knew I was up in the air, buckled in tightly and watching the planet from a tiny plane entering one of the largest canyons on earth. Now that's properly 'awesome'!

Leaving Wendell and Lorraine, I headed west towards Big Sur and the wondrous sites of the West Coast of America. Sadly Stanley Steamer Carpet Cleaner didn't cope too well with the slight detour into Death Valley National Park, so we grumbled gently along to

San Luis Obispo and meandered up along the coast road to San Francisco meeting pelicans, sea lions and sea otters along the way.

Having arrived in this eclectic city I was able to explore the magic of Chinatown, swing perilously from the back of a cable car and make flower garlands for random strangers in the Conservatory of Flowers in Golden Gate Park. Kindness begets kindness and, after all the truly special acts of kindness that I had enjoyed I really wanted to give back to others... even if it was by threading a few daisies through their hair.

I left this time in the USA with a host of wonderful experiences that have stood me in good stead in the world of B&B. I expected nothing and instead got the unexpected!

CHAPTER 2

Wishes DO Come True

'Be careful what you wish for' is an adage by which I have lived my life. We all know the story of someone who asked for more time to read, or more time to relax and then found themselves out of work or, worse still, out of the ability to work. If you get things that you desire, there may be unforeseen and unpleasant consequences. I am careful with wishes as they often come true!

I also firmly believe in the power of visualisation. Not that whimsical pie-in-the-sky notion of seeing things and making them jump into the palm of your hand, but the other sort of visualisation. The kind that empowers you to clearly see exactly what you want, how you will make it happen and how it will feel when you have it. Clear, concise, committed. As Bob Proctor says 'Thoughts become things', so why not choose the good ones?

*

In 2006 I had been living overseas for many moons and enjoying one of the most beautiful places in the world. Bermuda had been my home since, after recovering from a pretty rotten motorcycle accident, a random trip to see an old friend had landed me on its shores in 1990. I went for a two-week vacation on the way to visit my elder brothers in Texas. It seemed logical, in my world, to pop to this little island on my way across from the UK to the USA.

A tiny detour and I ended up staying for sixteen years! I fell hopelessly in love… with the island, its people and its magical air. Known as the Bermudas or Somers Isles, its nearest land mass is Cape Hatteras, North Carolina, USA, approximately 600 nautical miles to the north west. Its waters are an incredible azure blue and the sand is pink.

My only reference to this island group before landing there was the hype about the Bermuda Triangle, into which many have gone and been lost forever. I wasn't scared; I was intrigued. I was fascinated by the variety of hues that people had painted the outside of their houses. From dark red with even darker green shutters, to pale pinks and purples. Bright yellows and gentle blues, all with the crisp and clean whitewashed stepped roofs that so cleverly capture the rainwater for domestic use in a tank underneath the house.

I was charmed by the diversity of flora and fauna. From huge palm trees that dwarf humans and impressive banyan trees with their magical trunks and root systems to the more cultivated, but no less interesting, varieties of plants. Hydrangeas as big as doorways; freesias growing wild in people's lawns and on the edges of the road with their magical aroma pervading the air. Hibiscus and bougainvillea in more colours than I knew existed!

The birds in Bermuda also add to its rich tapestry. One of the locals, the Great Kiskadee, is renowned not only for its distinctive yellow, black and white colouring but also for its distinctive call which the locals suggest sounds like someone saying 'Where's my beer, where's my beer'! The Northern Cardinal brings a flash of bright red to the trees whilst the Eastern Bluebird can be sought out on golf courses and parks where volunteers monitor and maintain their bird boxes.

But the White Tail Tropic Bird, colloquially known as the Bermuda Longtail, is my favourite of all Bermuda birds. They are an open ocean species that only comes to land to breed and they only do this in Bermuda. These slender, graceful birds, whose arrival in February or March signifies spring, nest in single crevices and holes eroded from the soft limestone of Bermuda's coastal cliffs. Depictions of them are everywhere from bank notes to jewellery to T-shirts. They are a delight and I could often be found simply sitting on a pink, sandy beach watching them perform their airborne ballet.

Located in the Atlantic Ocean, Bermuda is in fact a crescent-shaped chain of 181 islands and islets that were once the rim of a volcano. According to locals, any patch of land that is more than twelve inches out of the water at high tide is an island. This means that only twenty of the islands are inhabited, although Bermuda is one of the most densely populated countries in the world.

But it's not the unique ecosystem or the indigenous and migratory birds that make it so special. It's not even the stunning, and I mean stunning, swathes of white and pink sandy beaches that make Bermuda such an enchanting place. It is in fact the people and the culture of this land that continue to make me delighted every time I return.

It is the absolute commitment to politeness that pervades the streets here. Pedestrians say 'Good day' to each other. Doors are held open, opportunities for kindness are relished and people smile when you enter a building. Failure to say 'Good afternoon' to other passengers, as well as the driver, when you get on the bus is a major faux pas.

Things enthral in Bermuda. Like the observance of absolute quiet on the main street on Remembrance Day. Like the exuberance of the crowds who use tape to mark out their space on the pavement a day ahead of the parade day to ensure they have their cooler and chair space to watch the entire procession, which encompasses traditional marching brass bands, baton-tossing jewel-bedecked dance troupes as well as the loud drum-ridden floats of reggae music.

Like the public and proud decision of the very dark-skinned gentleman who works at the petrol station to paint his 1954 split-screen Morris Minor shiny black to match his own colour. Like the colours of the dresses and the embracing of the cultures of Portuguese, African, Indian and English heritage and the unique way in which motorists say hello to each other and thank you for letting you in line by a wave of the hand and a toot on the car horn. The Bermuda driving test even has a question about when to use your horn: when passing someone, when making someone aware of potential danger or when saying 'hi' to your mates! The place is a hotspot of congeniality and it was no wonder that I went for two weeks and stayed sixteen years!

Whilst living in Bermuda, and visiting family in the UK, I met Miles. Tall, dark, handsome we clicked and started chatting on the phone, he in the UK and me in Bermuda. After £500 each on phone bills and some time spent together, we realised we really rather liked each other and had perhaps found that much sought-after soulmate.

*

I relocated to the UK and after a year of realising that we more-than-liked, we decided a new venture would be great for us both. As we all know, when you come out of a dark place in your life it's imperative to head towards a new brighter light. We had both had some tough life experiences, and so were keen to explore new ideas and dreams to see what adventures could be had. We banded together and threw up some ideas of where life would take us next.

Would we buy a traditional green narrowboat and live on the canal, with me writing the novel that's been inside whilst also creating new and interesting types of chutney, he running his natural stone business with just a laptop and a mobile phone?

Would we sell everything and take off to pastures new in Australia or New Zealand where the sheep outnumber humans and you can indulge the urge to wear a hat with corks hanging off it whilst uttering that unique greeting: 'G'day'?

Would we buzz off round the world in our iconic 1920s Tiger Moth biplane? With Miles as a qualified pilot at the helm and me as fabulous co-pilot (and no experience at all), we could circle the skies in search of adventure. Biggles goggles, white silk scarves flying diagonally and fat leather bomber jackets as our uniform, the sky was the limit!

YES… that's exactly what we decided… well, sort of…

*

What we actually did was start thinking about the plane that we pictured ourselves owning. We saw it clearly. Bright, shiny, poppy red; fabulous lines and the ability to give us complete freedom. Routes across continents were investigated and we considered how to learn wingovers and graceful barrel rolls in our new plane. Miles and I could feel the excitement and joy of independence already. We would fly and be free and write and adventure and be daring.

And then the other thoughts came… We thought about our families; mine older, his younger. We thought about having a place to have friends and family to visit. We thought about having a base from which we could adventure. This made sense as it has always been important to me to be financially secure; so we talked about a business that would give us freedom and income. A business that we could grow. How could we have our shiny red Tiger Moth plane whilst having a home and a business to sustain us?

Whilst we discussed and discovered and considered what to do, my thoughts often returned to my world-travelling days spent exploring Central and Southern Asia, America, Europe and Australasia. During these times I had stayed in wonderful hostels and B&Bs and my thoughts started to galvanise around the notion of a home-away-from-home like the ones I had experienced.

One of the most memorable hostels was The Pink House, perched high on a cliff overlooking Auckland harbour. This huge colonial-style house oozed congeniality and a light-hearted approach to life. Painted a gentle candy pink with large balustrades and deep verandas, it felt expansive and welcoming. Big comfy couches and funky recycled furniture was scattered about. An eclectic array of local artwork hung on the walls, alternative music was played and the whole place had an air of conviviality.

Memories from The Pink House made me feel warm. How would it be if we could create a place that we and our families could call home, but where we could greet people and offer them a warm and genuine welcome? I started to think about a bed and breakfast or something similar. Most of my travelling days I was on such a tight budget that it was hostels for me and as the time went by I realised that now into my forties, I didn't want a bunch of scruffy travellers (as I had been!) with smelly rucksacks and sandals coming to my house.

Whilst memories of The Pink House brought back great feelings, I knew also that time offers us a rose-tinted perspective of events and I had progressed a little further. I wanted a place with some finesse, nice carpets and good quality linens on the beds instead of sleeping bags, muddy boots and the smell of slightly dodgy socks pervading the air. This had been my travelling norm and I had loved my hostelling days, but I aspired to a more genteel way of life... or so I thought!

*

And so it was that on a sunny March day, Miles and I took ourselves off to the stunning Roman city of Bath, in the UK's south west corner. A rugby game lured us there and the city, which I had visited briefly before, shone its magnificent beauty once again. At the Bath rugby ground, affectionately known as 'the Rec' (recreation ground) with a lovely pint of Guinness in hand, Bath Abbey looming gently to the right, hills and woodland providing a wondrous backdrop, I thought I was in UK heaven!

That was early 2006. I still had the visualisation of the red Tiger Moth plane; the freedom; the meeting new people. Now added to this mix was the notion of hospitality and of creating a home for our families to enjoy. Confusion reigned!

So we started to bandy around the idea of a business that we could grow, where we could meet new and interesting people, where we could live but which would allow us long hours of flexibility so we could have our bi-plane and fly off to great adventures!… Why not look at running a B&B? More mothballs than Tiger Moths as it turns out, but who would have known?

Research online bought me to Caroline at oursource.co.uk. She suggested some property papers and contacts at some Bath estate agents, who I duly called. The information arrived and whilst enjoying a cuppa on a Monday morning while living in Miles' hometown of Horsham, we saw a house we liked. One hour later we were belting along the motorway towards Bath. Three hours later we were standing outside a gorgeous sixteenth-century guesthouse located in a picturesque village just outside Bath city centre. And that's when it happened… that's when our vision crystallised.

As we looked at the beautiful property that was for sale we saw the wisteria, dormant in winter but showing promises of beauty come springtime, we saw the quintessential medieval village around us… and there… swinging gently from its place on the side of the property clear as day, was the sign in bright poppy red: The *Plaine* Guesthouse.

We had found what we had visualised…

Our plane was the Plaine.

The sign was shiny red but there were no wings.

We knew then and there that this was our place and knew that our visualisation was complete. We had asked for something, hadn't stipulated that the plane needed wings and had been provided with an answer to many of our questions.

As Henri Frederic Amiel once said, 'Destiny has two ways of crushing us – by refusing our wishes and by fulfilling them.'

So… be careful. Dreams *do* come true so be careful what you wish for!

CHAPTER 3

Bollards

It's quite curious how we can get attached to inanimate objects. Like houses. And cars. And apparently bollards. Since moving to Norton St Philip and buying the ailing bed and breakfast at the centre of this village I had fallen hopelessly in love with the building, met upwards of 4,000 new faces in the first few years, cooked enough breakfasts to sink a battleship and cleaned my bathrooms until my fingers bled. I had also become quite attached to my bollards.

The definition of a bollard is a post that is put in the middle or at the end of a road to keep vehicles off or out of a particular area. Or, in this case, on the pavement outside a historic building in the UK to prevent traffic from mounting the pavement and mowing down pedestrians or hitting olde worlde walls.

These large, black metal mounds lined up on the pavement at the front of my home had been hit by lorries, tractors, cars and bikes so many times that the bill for black paint was getting out of hand! They were only supposed to be decorative! The home of which I speak is The Plaine, a sixteenth-century Grade II listed building situated in a picturesque village in quintessential South West England. This large imposing house is constructed of the soft, warm, honey-coloured stone that is typical of the Cotswolds and, with its many windows, boasts a prominent place in the village. It offers a refuge for travellers, a great photo opportunity for tourists and a home-away-from-home for those who stay here. The well-established and truly impressive slow-climbing wisteria growing across its front offers an abundance of pale mauve clumps of perfumed flowers and only adds to its charm. It makes you glad to be alive when you smell its aroma.

This is the scene five years on from my entry into the vim and vigour world of B&B. But this isn't where it all started... oh no!

This all started long, long ago (well, 1992), in the far-off land of New Zealand in an extraordinary travellers' hostel called The Pink House in Auckland. I had finally managed to get to this isolated Pacific island where the Kiwis live and the culture is largely inherited from British and European custom, interwoven with Maori and Polynesian traditions. Getting here via Australia had been an adventure of selling potpourri and dried flower bouquets door to door, waitressing on the beach in 95-degree heat, having to wear shoes that were too small and driving 1,100 kilometres in a camper named Poo across the famous Nullarbor Plain from west to east, crossing the border between South and Western Australia. But that's another story.

The Pink House was impressive. Large, airy rooms offered space to lounge about. The gardens were flowered, the hammocks swinging and the views exceptional. Deep, meaningful conversations about the plight of the dolphins happened at one end of the house, while a debate about Madonna's latest outfit (it was 1992 for heaven's sake) ranked highly at the other! Cards were played, dances danced, hugs shared, beers consumed and friendships made!

With twelve large rooms which slept upwards of twenty people per night in a selection of dorms and mixed rooms, and a reception area that catered for everything from sticky plasters to emergency international telephone calls (this was in the days before mobile phones and the internet), the racket and mayhem was colossal! But each morning when we, the lucky folk who stayed here, wandered downstairs bleary eyed it was often to follow the sound of voices offering a bit of toast, some Advil or cereal after another heavy night as travellers, everything was lovely and comfy again. And everyone who stayed there felt as though they were in seventh heaven! The gardens weren't littered with the beer bottles which had been 'forgotten' there the previous evening; the couches were plumped and ready to welcome us; the tables and chairs strewn around the previous evening had all been meticulously put back into their own casual space and the whole house was filled with fresh air and light. It was a truly marvellous place to relax for a few days whilst planning the next bit of my adventure round the islands of New Zealand. The rooms were light and airy, the beds clean, the owners chatty and knowledgeable and the guests all super fun!

Never once did it occur to me, or I suspect most of the other temporary residents, that things didn't miraculously straighten themselves in the night. There wasn't in reality an army of small, wand-waving fairies who ran around the place tidying cushions, placing cast-off articles of clothing in a safe place, emptying overflowing ashtrays and collecting abandoned beer bottles. The beds didn't miraculously make themselves, the gardens didn't weed themselves and the hostel reservations weren't made by telepathy. Food did not magic itself from the grocery store and the upkeep of the house wasn't done by elves. Nope, there was no such thing. Just a small army, actually three people, who worked round the clock at The Pink House to ensure we had a relaxed, chilled, hassle-free place to enjoy.

Never for a minute did it occur to me that they must work feverishly to keep things running, that the laundry mountain must be of gargantuan proportions, or that it took colossal effort to keep being polite and kind and reassuring to what must sometimes have been wet-behind-the-ears 'travellers' who actually needed babysitting. After all, it would only be the occasional request for an extra loo roll, wouldn't it? Only one of us that ever needed a quick run to the pharmacy as they had fallen over and got a deep cut; only we could ever be locked out after a night's bender and have to knock someone up to let us in at 3am. Yes, we presumed that we were actually the only ones in existence! The naïvety of it all – but looking back it was by far the most perfect place in which to stay and my memories of this lovely house are as affectionate today as they were during my stay.

*

After a few days of acclimatisation to the world of travelling 'down-under', I subsequently left The Pink House with a lovely naïve attitude about how the hostel had operated and continued my travels on and off for several years. I moved from continent to continent, but always had a soft spot for this big Pink House that offered solace and space and security. And somewhere lodged at the back of my mind was the absolute conviction that this would be a great thing to do. To be able to welcome people into my home, to offer them a super place to stay, have lively, lovely conversations and a feeling of well-being… yes! By doing this 'one day' I would be able to make a difference to people's lives as the good people at The Pink House had made a difference to mine. I would be that welcoming, witty, brilliant and engaging individual. I would provide a safe haven for the fearful and forlorn as well as the hopeless or homesick. I would repay previous kindness and be known for my generous nature! I would offer hugs and giggles and a helping hand!

It stands to reason then that I thought the B&B world would be about just this. I thought it would be just lovely opening the lovely front door to lovely people coming to stay at my lovely home in my lovely village. I thought that I would be the hostess with the mostest floating around the place chatting with guests, being a fabulous mixture of flowery kaftan-wearing Margo Leadbetter from that great British TV show *The Good Life* and flaky but lovely Edina in *Absolutely Fabulous*, entertaining people with interesting ditties about life. I pictured fabulous conversations over delicious meals in our dining room with the eclectic group of friends who would gather while the wine flowed and the candles twinkled.

I would be recommending my favourite places and telling amusing anecdotes about life, the universe and everything. I thought that 'beds and a bit o' brekky', which is what I perceived B&B life to be, must be so liberating. My thoughts ran something like this:

I'll have the beds all done and the rooms dusted before lunch so that I can spend my time reading, perhaps crocheting and going for long walks in the country with the golden Labrador who will live with me in this idyllic setting. I will be relaxed, have lots of friends and free time to enjoy them.

I thought B&B life would be fabulous. And it is!

And…

The journey was – and continues to be – interesting. Strangely enough the magical band of wand-waving, couch-plumping, garden-tidying fairies didn't come to live at my house any more than it did at The Pink House in Auckland! The garden did need weeding, the walls did need painting and people did ring the bell at ridiculous hours to be let into their rooms after a night on the town. The mountain of laundry, the tedium of routine, the confines of a small rural business and the challenges it presents all came at a cost.

But…

Along the way there have been some giggles, some tears, many hugs, some tough words, some light-bulb moments of realisation and some downright silliness! I have stared at bank statements that reflect nothing of the work I have done. I have changed beds at 11pm to accommodate late-arriving guests; I have endured a selection of unruly and sometimes feral children; I have listened to ailments, aches, pains and descriptions of disorders that would make many GPs blush! There have been stories of hope and bravery, faith and despair, as well as a remarkable amount of good heartedness and humour. I continue to polish, paint and prune to create my own special dream of hospitality and humour…

But before going into any of them, let's go back in time to a moment when the world of B&B was enjoying the simple pleasures of a romantic night away without knowing what chaos is going on in the background. Let's return to a time when I stayed at B&Bs and left with a smile and a happy full tummy! Let's return to sanity!

CHAPTER 4

Sanity and Love

There was a time when I had few or no ties. When I first met Miles we could roam freely and not have to be back for check-in time at 5pm. We once went to Brighton for the afternoon.

Watching rugby in a local pub I said, "Shall we just get drunk and stay the night?"

"Yes!" said G, and we did. We actually ended up staying two days. We checked into the B&B after popping to Woolworths to buy toothpaste and toothbrushes and a deodorant to share! Those were the days when I ate a full English with relish... whilst sitting down instead of having to jump up and check out a guest, or help find a lost key, or answer the door, or help with staff issues. There was a time when I would *stay in* instead of *running* a bed and breakfast! Oh the long-ago memory, and *no* regrets.

Miles and I had decided on a journey together and had visualised a plane to take us off on our travels. In the meantime we had seen a beautiful property for sale called the Plaine Guesthouse... fortuitous we thought; perhaps we could even call it fate? I believe in things happening for a reason, even when at the time we might not be able to understand them. I have a belief that the universe is unfolding exactly as it should and that a wee bit of faith is what's needed to see you through.

Anyone who has ever encountered a thing of beauty knows that deep, warm feeling that ensues. Maybe it's a special person, an amazing view or a piece of architecture. It's a feeling that you can't describe. It's a deep resonance with something that really fills your heart and makes you want to be around this beautiful thing more and more. It's a thing that makes you smile. And so it was for me when I first set eyes on the Plaine.

She (and yes I do know that she is a she) is a sixteenth-century house that makes you want to stay beside her and be her friend. She sits at the crossroads and dominates with her gentleness the small village of Norton St Philip in Somerset. Although now she has a façade that suggests Georgian roots, her heritage goes back to the time of Cromwell and fighting for honour, and the Pitchfork Rebellion of 1685.

She has seen much, changed many times and been home to hosts of people. According to folklore she has been two houses and had an army of the pseudo-intellectual Beatniks living there in the 1960s, one of whom had a pink Rolls Royce that she used to park outside the front. She was used as an antiques shop, a doctors' surgery and a shop as well as a place where gentlemen could pay for the indulgence of the company of women.

One of the ladies who worked with us remembers her aunt living in the house.

"She used to sit in her rocking chair in front o' that fire and tell people what ale they could 'ave," she told us. The fireplace is Jacobean and refreshments of ale and cider came from the small barrels that sat in the window.

"It was always warm and toasty in 'ere. Aunty kept a good space."

But it wasn't just the house that I was enamoured with. It was the whole village of Norton St Philip, which is steeped in history and really is an interesting place to see. The Plaine stands opposite the impressive thirteenth-century George Inn, and this junction became a major part of the stage coach route between London and South West England. On 12 June 1668 the noted diarist, Samuel Pepys, with his wife and servants, passed through Norton St Philip on their way to Bath from Salisbury.

The inn was later used as the headquarters of Monmouth's army, during the Monmouth Rebellion in 1685, after his retreat from Bath. In the aftermath of the failed rebellion, Judge Jeffreys used the George Inn as a courtroom and conducted twelve executions on the village common as part of the Bloody Assizes. This is interesting history, which spreads to The Plaine as it too was used as a hostelry for the lesser mortals of the entourages that travelled through the village.

Whilst the George got the high-falutin' members of the aristocracy and the old malt house next door apparently housed the ladies-in-waiting and manservants of the elite, it seems that we had the most fun-loving group as we had the wheeler-dealers, the tradesmen and the underlings who no doubt brought much character to The Plaine!

But it's not just her position that makes her so beautiful. It's the aura. She looked so calm and so welcoming that I was completely in love before we went inside. After many years of working for myself in business, I *know* you should never buy with your heart. I know I should have done lots of due diligence and I am fully aware that I should have looked at demographics, market research, other properties, created a business plan and done lots of other very sensible things. I have been a business coach for years… I should know this stuff! But I didn't, as I am afraid I fell totally in love, and reason left me!

Beams and uneven floors and large airy four-poster bedrooms with lots of chintz greeted us as we entered The Plaine. I looked at walls and décor and pictured guests arriving and how we would reconfigure the house. Miles pottered around muttering about electricity supply and hot-water lagging, underground mains supply and roof linings. We both enjoyed the sense of something new and exciting for us. Not for us the stern, sombre faces of professional buyers, which might have been our better approach, but instead a gleeful abundance of natural good humour, positive reactions and overwhelmingly nice comments. The estate agent had a field day!

"The garden is nice, isn't it?" he said.

"Yeeeeeeees," I cooed.

"The kitchen has a nice feel," he suggested.

"It does," I simpered.

"The downstairs toilet is all that it should be."

"Oh indeed it is!"

Pathetic really as all in all I was a bargain-hunter's nightmare and an estate agent's dream. We loved the Plaine and it showed.

*

So we came, we saw, we stayed, we went to the pubs, we walked round the village and then we reluctantly went home to do some sums! It was going to take everything we had and then some, but we made it happen. It took time, blood, sweat and tears before we finally got the right mortgage at the right rate with the right repayments. But we did it and we celebrated when the offer was accepted, celebrated when our mortgage was approved and then sat in absolute shock when we actually realised the enormity of the project!

I worried that it was my dream and not that of this fella I had only known for a little while. I worried about my ability to create the ambience that I knew was needed to take the business further. I worried a *lot*. And who could blame me?

Let's have a quick look at my experience in the hospitality industry. Hummmm, OK, so I have been a waitress serving pizzas and beer in a rowdy British-style pub called the Robin Hood in

Bermuda. I have waitressed on beaches in Northern Australia to finance my combi van as I travelled round the amazing land of Oz.

There have been various stints at bartending, washing up, organising parties and events. Oh yes, and I once worked for Trusthouse Forte in North Yorkshire. I had run away from my Midlands home to join a circus. I joined up to play with miniature motorcycles and create fun events in the arena outside the circus tent (which had no live animals, I must add). It was fun, until the relentless rain became too ugly and muddy and the small folk didn't want to play on miniature motorbikes! So I found myself in North Yorkshire without a job or friends or a place to live. So I rented a room for a week and strolled up and down the beautiful high street of Northallerton, the county town of North Yorkshire.

I was offered bar-tending jobs, a hostess position, waitressing and even a sweeper-upper job in a hair salon. But when I entered the Golden Lion Hotel on the high street I met with Mr Jacobs, the manager, who happened to be behind the reception desk.

"Good day," I said. "Do you have any staff vacancies please?"

"Do you have any experience?" he asked.

"Well, to be honest, now you come to ask, in so many words… no!" I finally replied.

"Right, come and have tea in my office." And away I was whisked.

Strange way of doing things, I thought, but OK, so off we went. After about fifteen minutes he offered me the job of waitress, which I eagerly accepted. It was full time and the pay sounded good. Then he told me that he also needed a deputy manager who would be required to live in the manager's suite on site, he told me about the perks of the job and that I could start the next day. It was his assertion that I obviously had balls to come and look for work as I had and that was the kind of person he needed on his team. Not some, in his words, "namby pamby wet-behind-the-ears-jumped-up-college-graduate-who-knows-nowt!"

It seemed rude not to accept and so my adventures into hospitality commenced. I learnt more in six months about hospitality and attitude than I could ever have learnt at any college. Mr Jacobs once explained to me that the reason for hiring me wasn't my ability; it was my attitude. He said that people could learn process but not personality. For that feedback I am forever grateful, as it has stood me in great stead to enter places where others might feel trepidation. I don't fear the unknown, I embrace it and I don't worry that things won't turn out OK, because they do.

That is why I didn't worry about the people who would come to this beautiful building and stay with us and allow us to have a business we enjoyed so much. I didn't worry about the lovely times we were going to have here because I had an innate and absolute belief in humanity and that it would all work out beautifully.

*

Now, there have been buckets of tears, gorgeous amounts of laughter, immense tiredness and fabulous people to meet and greet. There have been many, many times when we wondered how it was all going to come together, but we also kept clear in our visualisation and kept on finding new ways to bring more people to stay with us. We took a punt. On ourselves and our ability. We believed that we could turn the business from merely paying its way (just) to being reputable, economically viable, sustainable and flourishing. And we did, but what we learnt along the way has been invaluable, encouraging and enlightening.

We have witnessed connections being made; memories created and have seen how people interact with each other in a variety of ways. I have always believed in human nature as being inherently good and charitable. Yes of course that has been severely tested on some occasions but it will never dampen my belief in people and their ability to care. Owning a B&B gives an insight into a magnificent array of interactions and I have been able to 'people watch' without invading personal space. Words and body language are often not allied and by being able to stand back and observe, I have learnt much about people, communication and foibles. There is one thing that stands out though and that is that people truly are compassionate. Most people do feel empathy for others and I have witnessed great kindness whilst owning this fine house. The journey has been an adventure to say the least and I love the memories that keep me giggling and smiling and sharing!

CHAPTER 5

Chintz and Geraniums

Whoever said that combining chintz and pink, flowery wallpaper borders and geraniums was a good idea? What crazed interior designer-type person thought this arrangement would bring finesse and add beauty to a stunning medieval home? When did someone say, 'Gosh, I know a styling suggestion for this beautiful B&B. I will gather together lots of flowery, fussy fabric, put it together with bits of ruffly, ribbony, tacky stuff, add some nasty dried flowers and put it everywhere? I shall then adorn this four-poster bed with an excess of ruffles, bows and round frilly cushions but why stop there? Why not add borders on the walls, borders in the bathrooms, borders at waist height and borders at picture rail height?'

I feel 1983 is the answer and I hold the entire year responsible for some dreadful style options. Shoulder pads, matching electric blue earrings, belt and shoe sets, exercise gear worn outside of the gym, Magnum PI-style Hawaiian shirts and the onset of the curly perm, to name but a few.

But these fashion faux pas aside, back at the B&B I found not just a border of a different colour, but a veritable smorgasbord of borders. One room held a thick pink border with stripes emanating from the bottom, intermittent different pink flowers in the middle with a totally different colour, shade and dimension of flower on the top. Another room had been favoured with a teal and pink concoction of birds, flowers and intertwined twigs through the pattern, with, yes you've guessed it, a border in a different colour!

When we moved into the house in late November 2006, we had completely fallen in love with the place. I have been down that road of blissful ignorance before. That road that comes with the first flushes of new love. It's the place where you don't see any pitfalls. You see only the beautiful and wonderful things that blind you with their magnificence. You bask in the wonders of this new love and refuse to see the glaringly obvious challenges that face you head on!

Yes, that's exactly what happened with the Plaine. We didn't really *see* the décor, we didn't really *see* the chintz and border-trimmed bedrooms with carpets that had known better days and the over-laden four-poster beds with their cream, lacy, slightly ripped and slightly darned edges. We didn't see the once-upon-a-time sunshine yellow hues of the dining room walls with its heavy dark-blue drapes and double lamps in the shape of chandeliers that bumped your head as you walked past. In the guest lounge, we didn't really see the small, round, faded chintz cushions that were on the chintz couches in the chintz room under the chintz curtains on the chintz carpet!! Funny how love makes you blind. And we definitely didn't notice the abundance of geraniums, with their lemony-green-rose grandmother smell everywhere!

So, it took a couple of months whilst we were getting used to our beautiful new home but then we realised it was time to take a good hard look at the love of our life, the Plaine. It was time to really look and potentially, just potentially, see the foibles, the idiosyncrasies and the changes that needed to happen in and to our beloved. Oh, and what changes there were! Fundamentally she was still the gorgeous home we fell in love with… that didn't change. She is built of that honey-coloured Cotswold stone that changes shade with the seasons and the light. She has great proportions and the rooms are light and airy. But, and it's rare I use the word… but, she did need a small amount of cosmetic surgery: a little facelift to bring her back to her full potential; maybe not even surgery, perhaps just a flash of lippy and some mascara! Whatever it was she needed, she needed it soon!

*

I had seen a transformation in another B&B years before. This was on a trip to Stone Mountain near Atlanta, Georgia. I had decided to take my parents on a road trip from Boston to Texas, so obviously we went via Atlanta! The wrinklies and I have been on many road trips and we tend to simply go where the wind takes us, or, in this case, a rather nice American car with air-con and reclining seats. Texas was home to two of my siblings for a while so it seemed reasonable to take a week and drive across the States to see them.

When we arrived at Stone Mountain it was agreed that we perhaps weren't going to take up the various offers of snowboarding (indoor and out), mountain climbing (with ropes or without), fishing, hiking or golfing as my parents, then in their seventies, are more the pottering, lingering, chatting-to-antique-shop-owner type of travellers. So that's what we did, and Stone Mountain does not let you down with its menagerie of 'antiques', collectables and craftsy stores; it was just what they wanted.

We then found the Village Inn, which had been one of the original houses in the area and had been lovingly restored by the new owners. They had recreated what's known as the Folk Victorian architectural style with exposed rafters, porches supported by massive wood or brick pillars and windows delicately organised into pairs.

We were enchanted by the history and the photos of the renovation: a mammoth task but they had done it. What they had also done was to create individual rooms, which were bespoke and completely unique. They were all themed in the slightly Disney-like-over-the-top but brilliant way only the Americans can do!

Delores, our very own Southern Belle and the owner, introduced each one to us.

"This here is the Scarlett Room," she drawled, as she opened the door into the den of reds, dark maroons and sultry lighting. A boudoir of the first order!

"As you'all know this is in respect for our beloved *Gone With The Wind*," she said reverently. "The Angel Room is our special place for our winged friends to gather. It has a Jacuzzi corner bath that our Angels approve of for relaxation," she said, showing us the next room. This room was duck-egg blue and white and was festooned with the cherub-faced icons, who watched over you from every corner.

Delores was justifiably proud of the Rhett Room. It was impressive beyond words with its collection of large portraits of a certain Mr C. Gable on several walls, including one opposite the throne! The four-poster bed was hunky, tall, dark and handsome and needed a small set of stairs to access it.

Finally, there was the fascinating-but-I-couldn't-sleep-a-night-in-it Civil War Room, which housed enough star-spangled banners, weaponry, Confederate flags, and armoury to start the whole thing again! The renovation was a labour of love and it offered a window into what people can do when they set their minds to it. I didn't know about my beloved Plaine then, but I respected the belief of the owners who knew that they were custodians of a special place in history, and that they were duty bound to look after it.

We also knew that the Plaine was, and is, a special piece of England's history, as are any of our over 374,000 listed buildings. We have a duty to care for and protect these parts of our heritage for future generations.

*

But back to my beloved Plaine, and to be honest the start of the makeover happened the second morning we were there! In our rush to meet our guests and impress them with our happy bouncy spirit (see the following chapter on Labrador tendencies) we were downstairs in the main rooms by 6.30am the day after we moved in. We wandered from room to room and looked and giggled and went 'eek' and put our hands over our mouths in gleeful anticipation of what we were embarking upon. And that's when I saw it. The fan. Not since 1982 had I seen one of these. A light-brown rattan fan: flat, dust-laden with a menagerie of dried flowers that had had their last bloom circa 1972. It was *horrid*. And like with many things, when you have seen one you simply keep seeing bad things! I saw the fake Portuguese embroidered tablecloth, the metal table with expanding wooden legs that someone had brought back from their holiday in Turkey and thought it would go beautifully in the sitting room of an English home. I saw the small china dogs with the sad eyes and chipped noses. I saw the glass vase with the fake flower and, worse still, the fake water.

And luckily village life in rural England continues undaunted with jumble sales on a regular basis. Thank heavens for that!

"Would you like some donations?" I asked the lady at the first village hall.

"Yes dear, have you got much?" I don't think she had reckoned on a carload but she gratefully took the offending items. Things were transported to another smaller hall in a village several miles away, sometimes under the cover of darkness so that I wouldn't offend the previous owners.

It was Operation Clean Sweep. And cathartic. I felt I was giving my love a new lease of life! But the wall chintz was everywhere and it couldn't be disguised. Through the hall, the stairs, the landings, even in a small bathroom. It was overwhelming and I couldn't bear it any more.

I craved blank walls with soft edges, colours that were restful instead of argumentative, a blank canvas upon which to put art... I just wanted it to be *plain*!

And so the painter came and whistled, painted and hummed while I moved things and ran to Homebase. And he whistled and painted and I wandered through catalogues and painted with him and whistled with him and agonised!

Was it the right shade?

Would the vibrant red on a hall wall welcome or offend?

Would it in fact all be too plain?

Would the newly revamped bathroom work or look too modern?

Did the white walls and no curtain option in the dining room really enhance its natural beauty?

Would I regret the facelift?

Nope... not a bit... not for a minute!

*

She looked marvellous. I can't say ten years younger, because that was definitely not the objective; but by the end of three months, and in time for our first season to begin, she looked serene and peaceful and happy again. Her windows were painted so that her eyes could regain their sparkle. Her walls were covered with gentle stone tones that are warm in winter and refreshing in the summer; her bathrooms welcomed you as did the red wall as you opened the front door into the hall. Well, it was fabulous! Blossoms of every colour flowed from the pots at the front of house as the joy of winter pansies never ceases to amaze me. The geraniums were rehoused to some of the older members of the village and the chintz was gone.

So even though curtain tiebacks are a ridiculous sum of money, and paint is the price of gold, I knew it had all been worth it because it created a really exciting space.

Ready for a new season.

Ready to meet and greet crowds of new potential friends.

Ready to enjoy B&B land with this beautiful home resplendent!

A facelift on humans can be a snub in the face of nature's breathtaking work, but a little 'help' on this old property made her even more of an attractive place for people to come and stay. To this day, people will walk into rooms and say that they are relaxing or peaceful or simply nice. And that's a super feeling to have from a lot of hard work, and a mile away from chintz and geraniums.

CHAPTER 6

Unleash the Labradors

When you first take over a bed and breakfast business, the realisation of your dream, you are naturally a little excited… trepidatious, but excited. We had been dreaming, planning, scheming and packing and finally the day arrived for us to get all our belongings safely along the M4 and deposit them in Norton St Philip at The Plaine. One large van was all it would take. We were sure. We didn't have *that* much gear really. Until we realised that the 'small' self-storage unit was actually larger than we remembered and all of that 'stuff' in it needed to go with us.

Norman, the quietly spoken Yorkshire van man turned up a little early as he explained, "'Tis a long way to Bath. Thee will have to make haste to get there afore dark."

It was 8am; plenty of time, we thought.

Norman was perfectly calm as we diligently loaded boxes, couches, shelves and plants. He was confident.

"'Tis a good van this. It'll tek a whole 'ouse full o' stuff."

He was less keen when we produced a full-size fridge freezer that had been hiding in the back of the unit and proceeded to wedge it into his truck.

He was still less impressed when, as the boxes wouldn't fit, we started to take out duvets and cushions and stuff them into any corner of his truck that was or was not available. He humphed a little, groaned a little and showed his dissatisfaction at the situation with a hearty "Eeeeeee, that's a struggle in't it."

And it was, but we made it and with Norman in front we were ready for the off.

*

Horsham, in West Sussex, had been our home for a while and Miles and I both had cars into which we could stuff more 'stuff'. And so it was that we propelled ourselves in convoy down the long stretch of the M4 to our new home. There is a car park at the back of the house in which we presumed we would unload. And we could.

What we hadn't remembered were the stairs/steps. Not lots of them and not huge staircases up which we had to climb. Instead just a variety of sizes, all on different levels, and many opening into doorways made for those of a small stature. Not made for twentieth-century people, these doors were cut for small furniture made of tree wood and whittled to fit doorways. They were created for people whose average height might have been five foot three, instead of the nearly six-foot people who were now arriving! So, several hours later, a plethora of trips up and down stairs, some choice words upon continually bashing heads on low beams and unexpected hunks of stone, finally we had an empty Norman van and a very full owners' quarters at The Plaine!

We waved off Norman, whose parting words were; "Good luck to thee. It'll tek a month o' Sundees to get yoursen clear. But good luck young 'uns!"

*

It's sobering to see the amount of 'things' that people collect whilst travelling through life, isn't it? Some are understandable. The kitchenware, the bedding and pictures. Some you relate to. For me the boxes of photo albums that represent so many trips in a lifetime make perfect sense. These to peruse when I have time and someone to share them with. Photo albums are about the journey, so mine are created with much love and the addition of anecdotes, bus tickets, maps and random thoughts on the places I visit. Strangely, with the invention of digital cameras I find my albums are less eclectic as I print less and less off the camera and rely instead on storage in a 'cloud' or memory stick. How much better it is to actually see a collection of photos and memories in an album rather than rarely opening the folder marked 'Pictures' on your computer.

However, there are things that people accumulate which I simply don't get. Miles had a plethora of these. Who needs a *Star Wars* figurine that someone else's son gave *his* son when they were six (now nineteen) and which has a broken wand thing (yes I know The Force will now get me!)? Who needs a pair of deck shoes, which are clearly two sizes too small but which you have had forever and that you might wear one day (when you have your toes amputated). And what about that old chestnut, the box of aftershaves which has probably been travelling around with you through the last six house moves but which you feel compelled to hold onto as they were expensive. The fact that their smell probably resembles a combination of slightly soggy rose petals, vinegar and cheese seemed to have bypassed Miles so we transported them all to the new abode.

After dumping all our gear and creating enough space to move about, we explored our new home. Nine bedrooms, six bathrooms and us rattling around playing house. The previous owners had left us plenty of food for the two guests that we had inherited with the business. A lovely couple from Malta had been staying for three days and their last vacation days would be with us. We were delighted and excited and very keen to meet them. So off we toddled to bed in order to get up bright-eyed and bushy-tailed like the brilliant new B&B owners we were!

So, at precisely 6.15am we both sprang out of bed and hurried downstairs to our new kitchen to work out how everything came together, where all the pots were and how we needed to lay a table. We were gleeful and kept sharing secret smiles as we found things and did little dances of joy at the discovery of a whisk… ooooo! or a frying pan… good gracious! And joy of joys: matching placemats!

It really was quite silly but by 8am we had sausages cooked, bacon waiting, mushrooms, beans and all the trankelments (old Black Country word) of a full English breakfast ready for our unsuspecting guests. Jamie Oliver would have been proud. We kept bacon moist in foil and mushrooms gently sautéing whilst plates were warmed under the grill. We had new pinnies on and were about to burst with excitement when the poor souls came into the dining room. We were unable to hold ourselves in check.

"Hello, I'm Miles," he said, wringing the gentleman's hand vigorously up and down.

"Hi, I'm Stephanie, we're delighted you are here," I gushed and beamed.

We resembled two over-sized, over-excited Labrador puppies bounding around telling them how wonderful it was to meet them and what an honour it was to have them to stay and the sheer joy of their arrival. I can picture them now: these quiet folk gently retreated towards the wall nodding with hands outstretched in front of them as if trying to calm a completely deranged lunatic until the cavalry would come and save them.

The cavalry never came and we showed them to their table. We explained about the breakfast, which of course they already knew having been there for a few days anyway. We ran and skipped to the kitchen and prepared a lake-full of fresh coffee, yards of toast, white and brown and proceeded to bring them the entire contents of the fridge. The plates were piled high with an abundance of food, which we presumed they would think was fabulous and be delighted with our creation. Instead they both politely turned their faces towards us and quietly said, "This is all perfectly lovely and thank you for your trouble but we really only want some cereal and toast this morning please. And sorry to disappoint you but could we have some tea?!"

"Yes, yes of course," we enthused and we were off. Me to get fresh tea and cups and saucers and Miles to ensure all manner of marmalades and jams were on offer. With this done we looked at each other and then looked at the heaps of food. It clearly would have been ridiculous to waste such an array of fabulous plated ingredients. So, like true warriors we sat in the kitchen away from our guests, and ate the lot. We wolfed it down then sat back and thought, well, what a jolly jape.

"This is gonna be great," said Miles, an ex-rugby player who loved his food. "We get to eat a full English breakfast each day."

The downside of this is that we continued to eat like this for many weeks, thinking that it was just acclimatisation. We also had a few too many visits to the local pub, which resulted in additional pounds on the waist. It never occurred to us (or we decided denial was a happy place to be) that it could possibly be detrimental to us to eat an F.E.B each morning. Several years on and several sizes bigger it would appear that the full English breakfast diet isn't actually best for the waistline. We were delighted to be able to have such an abundance of food, but once again we were reminded to be careful what you wish for!

Thomas and Mary, as we finally found out our first-ever guests were called, had been to stay at the Plaine many times before. They were fond of the area and had made some good friends in the village over the years. They have also been back to stay several times with us… which is good… as it means that, contrary to my early worryings, we didn't put them off completely and they loved us despite the Labradorian antics!

CHAPTER 7

I Love to Clean!

Or rather I love to see the results of cleaning and like to have a dirt-free environment. But the actual cleaning, the hoovering, the dusting, the moving things and the scrubbing bit of cleanliness? Nope, it's really not for me. As someone once said, "Housework can't kill you but why take the chance?" But, when you have a business based on people coming to stay with you then there is a genuine need for a little OCD attention to detail.

But it's like painting the Forth Bridge, isn't it? Cleaning I mean.

And it doesn't matter whether you have a studio apartment or a nine-bedroom house. Just when you think you have vacuumed, polished, dusted, buffed, scoured and generally beautified every single surface in your home, you look around and there they are: lurking… the dreaded dust bunnies or cobwebs or little bits of lint that were simply hovering threateningly ready to pounce and descend onto your perfect floor. It's that tiny smudge on your polished surfaces or the smear left on the window when you sit down to have a much-deserved cup of tea. They mock you with their tenacity and refusal to budge! This is no more noticeable than in the cleanliness-necessitating world of the B&B. I have spent days, weeks, months and what actually feels like years ensuring that each and every room is perfect and lovely, and all just in time for a little bundle of fluff to make its wretched way to the floor, all expertly timed for just when my new guests arrive.

It matters not that the duster was just in my hand, or that I had managed to squirrel the can of polish away in an unsuspecting jug. It only matters that there will always be, by some amazing cosmic power, a bit of fluff which is eminently visible, that catches the guest's eye and makes me very uncomfortable!

How many times have I screamed on the inside, *NO! NO! Please don't judge me on this, the rest of house is perfect. It's just the bit you can see that's dusty… honest! It's just a bit o' fluff.*

Then they go into the recently sterilised buffed sanctum that will be their resting place for the nights to come and what happens? Yep!… Geoffrey (*and they are all called Geoffrey*) spider has decided to throw himself off a perfectly good surface and create a beautifully intricate lattice-like creation between the taps on the otherwise gleaming sink.

And it's not because the guests actually say anything. They don't need to. It's as if they read your mind and know that you are cowering inside and then there is that imperceptible and very nearly inaudible sigh of disappointment. A slight 'huhhhhh'. It's a miniscule silent nod of disapproval from your new arrival and once again you howl inside at the injustice of it all. You had just been in the room, you had seconds before surveyed to ensure no Geoffreys were about; and yet they have snuck out in those few minutes, wreaking what you think of as havoc in your guests' room. I am sure they don't mean it. I am sure they don't maliciously plan their revenge for you obliterating their once-perfect web with a swish of your duster. I am sure they don't wait in anger wringing their tiny paws (do spiders have paws?) together in anticipation of their next planned attack. I am sure they don't simply go to sleep in the day so that they can furiously knit their fabulous webs in the dead of night, ready for you to find after your cleaning frenzy.

No, that would be silly to think any of those things…

And perhaps just a little bit paranoid!

But heck, that's just another part of the wonder that is B&B land.

And what's *really* interesting is other people's perspectives on that bit o' fluff. I have made some lovely connections with people over the years of running the Plaine with candid, honest, open and downright forthright conversations having been one of the biggest bonuses. Some of these have been around fluff: let me explain. I am constantly trying to find ways to add more value to the customer experience at the Plaine. I strive to give each guest a good time, and this includes being very particular about cleanliness and tidiness etc. However, and I find this interesting, while there are some people who will pick up on the bit o' fluff there are many, many more will not see it as they are too busy looking at the space, or the comfort or the décor, or simply enjoying the congeniality of a somewhat different kind of landlady than either they were expecting who they might have encountered before. We are so busy chatting and laughing and enjoying meeting each other that the bit o' fluff is ignored and plays no part in their experience. And I think this could be said of life. When we are looking for fault or discrepancy or negativity we will no doubt find it. Similarly if we are looking for happy circumstances or feel-good moments, we will find them as well.

I know this is true and I have used this exercise many times with people to make this point. If you think of the colour green and then you keep looking for green things around you, they will pop up everywhere even though you had never thought of them before. Take a moment and look around. Look for green. It's everywhere and yet not until you focus on it do you realise how much is around you. And it's the same with positive or negative experiences, isn't it? If we constantly look for negative to justify a negative attitude then no doubt that's exactly what we will find. However, when we look for positives the same rule applies.

Whatever we focus on expands; good, bad or indifferent. And whatever we want in our lives, we can bring more to ourselves. We simply need to change where we put our focus.

I always share this at workshops that I teach on using laughter as an exercise (more on that later). I put this homework to them prior to our next meeting. I ask them to look for signs of happiness. Smiles, hugs, giggles, laughter, or whatever it is that represents happiness. Once they start looking and focusing on these things they find that they have an abundance of it in their lives. And then guess what? Most people feel the need to add to it. To smile more, to engage more, laugh a little more. This changes their levels of serotonin, increasing the blood-flow to their brains and helps their endorphins to work better, thus creating a more resourceful, more positive state. All by simply changing their focus. So whilst some people can focus on the bits o' fluff in life, I for one choose to enjoy the experience of life by focusing on the good stuff, not the bad.

We are surrounded by marvels every day and, to be honest, if there is a small web in your house, instead of worrying about it long into the night, simply enjoy: it's Mother Nature at her best.

CHAPTER 8

An Inspector Calls

As all good little B&Bers, and those who watch *The Hotel Inspector* and *Four In A Bed* reality TV shows will know, in order to be on the National Tourism Board website in the UK you must first have applied for, and received at some point soon after buying the business, a grading from either the AA (Automobile Association with the yellow sign) or QIT (Quality in Tourism with the red rose sign). I investigated both and decided that QIT was simply a prettier sign and I liked it. Well, there was a *little* more thought, such as price, but to be honest not a lot. Both schemes demanded the same standards of care and due diligence, and both set out criteria which any establishment must adhere to in order to be awarded (even though you pay for it!) your merit of stars. The range is one star to five stars. The average for most B&Bs is three to four stars, as in order to have a five-star rating, you must provide things like twenty-four-hour guest service and an elevator and robes and little slippers for each guest, which would be excessive for my establishment. For me it would be amazing and gratifying to meet the four-stars standard.

The criteria are clear and focus on the overall cleanliness and condition of the property, physical and personal comfort, hospitality of staff, attention to detail and an overview of the entire guest experience. The awarding of four stars is rigorous and what I aspired to have as a representation to the world of my standards of care. So once it was decided from which board we would seek approval, there commenced a period of anxiety and apprehension, which came to be affectionately called 'Inspector Alert'.

The paperwork was filed. The letter came advising me that I would be 'visited' and 'assessed' and that only after this would I find out what grade I had made. There would be no prior knowledge of the inspector's visit. It made me feel as though I was a criminal being marked down for the parole board after committing the heinous crime of purchasing a bed and breakfast. I knew I wanted the stars, but I was jittery for weeks in the run up to 'the visit'. However, I had started the process and knew that I needed a good grade, and so it was time to study the manuals of expectations and work out ways to exceed them. We had no idea when or where or how the inspector would appear, but we knew we had to be ready for the unexpected. I gathered my merry band of helpers, all three of them, and we decided on a strategy. "Pillow plumping," shouted Rachel.

"Lightbulb polishing and turning mattresses," said Jane.

"A new iron to create proper military-style creases," piped up Julie, whose hubby was in the army!

We would need to be even more diligent than usual as we had no idea when the inspector would arrive. Jane, our short, stocky, broad Glaswegian part-time helper perceived our inspector to be an "'Eavily disguised, mackintosh-clad, slightly dodgy character potentially smelling of old whisky. He will have been living out of a battered old suitcase for weeks on end so t'will be easy to spot him."

And had we been looking out for that we would have been sorely disappointed. Our dodgy out-to-make-us-slip-up inspector turned out to be quite the opposite. She was a lovely lady called Helen who had shoulder-length hair, wore a selection of clothes from the Per Una range of M&S, came from Macclesfield and liked Lily of the Valley perfume! Who would have guessed?

However, during the period of expectancy what we *did* know was that we were on tenterhooks! We all knew that we needed to be totally on the ball and that every booking must be treated even more diligently than usual. I was having so much fun running the B&B that answering the phone with a smile was second nature, but as with all humans we sometimes don't do everything exactly as we should. I might have not sent the confirmation email within twenty-four hours, I might not have taken down every dietary requirement and worse still I might not have offered dinner reservations for the guest. But what I *did* offer was a genuine welcome by phone, email or in person and that, I needed to remind myself, is what this business is all about.

During Inspector Alert it was difficult to relax. It's a crazy time when every fold of every napkin could be construed as inattentiveness and marked down and individual egg yolks counted. Each slight error of judgement might be found out, and if the loo roll hasn't got that particular triangle edge to it that was customised by Marriott Hotels in the seventies and has never been reneged upon, well, heavens knows what might happen!

In retrospect it was nuts! In retrospect I went over and above anything that was required and ended up getting myself into a real old tizz at the very notion that the inspector would not adore my beautiful home where I had worked so hard to create an abundance of charm and warmth.

In retrospect perhaps the stars didn't matter that much. But let me tell you, at the time it was imperative and urgent and all consuming!

And the worst bit: you simply never know when they are coming.

I had been told by a very reliable source that a one-night mid-week stay could offer the clue to an inspector. But we had many mid-week one-night stays and we wanted to make sure we provided the best customer service we could possibly offer on a consistent basis. We are all human but the thought of messing up on that very, very special day with that very, very special person was a strain worse than the onset of an impending wedding.

I found myself dressing up each morning with make-up and everything! And then polishing the tops of lightbulbs with a relentlessness that really was quite worrying. The toilet bowls in the house were places of beauty, gleaming inside and out; the inside rims cleaned with a special toothbrush each day.

I stood outside in the middle of a storm looking at the house to get a 'first impression'. For heaven's sake, she is a sixteenth-century house with oodles of class. Of course she makes a great first impression!

The carpets were re-vacuumed not long after the first morning clean.

The sheets were re-ironed while on the beds.

The skirting boards were sterile enough to eat off.

The four-posters were immaculate.

The cat that once in a while wanders through our garden was groomed, much to his chagrin.

Everything was more perfect than usual, cleaner than a hospital theatre and more tense than a first night performance!

Ironically, when she came and stayed and ate and chatted over breakfast... I didn't think anything of it... simply another lovely guest at the Plaine. But no – as she signed her cheque and I saw a business expense account a flurry of bother came over me.

Could it be?

Had it been?

Arrrgghhh, what had I done wrong?

She, who is now called SHE, booked a one-night stay as predicted. She was given all the right information and a great rate. She was advised of check-in times and it was agreed that she would be with us around 5.30pm. She arrived with a small suitcase and an averageness about her, which probably helped to get her the job in the first place. Average in a gentle, non-descript kind of way. She was of average height with average hair and wore average shoes and spoke with an average tone of voice. She asked all the same questions as many before her about the age of the house, the distance to Bath and other places of interest as she was shown to her four-poster bedroom. Little did I know that behind those closed doors she was actually putting on white gloves and running them over every surface. She was actually taking all the linen off the bed to check the mattress and she was putting her hands around the inside rim of my toilet. What a job, eh?

So by the time lovely Helen the inspector had come in for breakfast and chosen her cereal and yoghurt and then been presented with what I am actually proud to call a bloomin' good brekky, it was too late for me to change any first impressions and too late to worry about her experience.

Too late now, came the little voice as we shook hands for her to leave.

Too late to grovel about anything overlooked.

Too late to apologise for the toast not being perfect or the windows not sparkling – too late.

After paying by cheque, Helen then needed to 'come clean'. She handed her business card over with what could only be described as a kind and gentle smile and said, "Well, I have been just a little bit sneaky. You might have been expecting an inspector. And here I am."

At this point I came undone. All the weeks of pressure exploded like an old-fashioned pressure cooker and this usually calm and sometimes even collected person simply burst into a volume of noisy tears. I was a blubbering mess for a few moments then collected myself, made sweet tea and sat with her while we walked through the ups and downs of my precious B&B. We talked duvet tog weights, teacups, mattress strengths and bath mats. We talked about organic local produce and type fonts for information sheets. We talked about Standard Operating Procedures to create an easy environment for my workers, all of which is grand but *really*?

Did she really need to keep me in such suspense? All I really wanted to know was that elusive promise of stars!

What had we achieved?

When could we have the shiny sign?

When could we pat ourselves on the back or I kick myself up the bum?

When could we all relax a wee bit?

Finally she uttered those unforgettable words, "We will be awarding you four STARS!"

Four stars, she said. Not even close to three as our standards were really very high, but never will be five unless you offer twenty-four-hour room service. Not likely, said I. We'll take the four thank you.

So the inspector came and the inspector gave and the strain of it is as clear a memory today as it was then! But it also raised questions for me about what hospitality actually is when it must be graded and standardised.

According to the *Oxford English Dictionary* the definition of hospitality is: 'The act of being friendly and welcoming to guests and visitors'. This of course applies to most places you would expect like hotels, guesthouses and bed and breakfasts. But not always, and not always to the same degree and not always with congruency and genuineness. Many people have stayed at The Plaine, and many have left with hugs and a smile and promises of returning to see us, or of recommending us to friends and family. But still more have said that we offer a home-away-from-home, a sanctuary, a gentle space to relax in. They have felt the humour and shared the laughter and been made to feel special. And it's those differences that cannot be conveyed through a series of tests or grades or standards. They are heartfelt and genuine, and they are what I am most proud of in this business. The team and I make a difference and that's the most wonderful feeling in the world. When someone recognises that you have improved their world it makes your heart soar, and the relentless piles of laundry and late-night phone calls seem worthwhile.

So perhaps today we can all share a bit of gratitude for those little things that happen in everyday life. Maybe we could be more friendly and welcoming to our guests, whether they are strangers we don't know, visitors from other lands or people we acknowledge on the street. I wonder how much kinder our world will be when we all take a few minutes just to recognise kindness or offer a little ourselves.

CHAPTER 9

Offspring, Children, Rug-rats, Kids

One of the very best things in life for me is the art of the hug. There are many varieties of hug including the 'A' line hug where two people stand a body-width apart, lean in and put arms round each other with a space in between them forming an 'A'; the buddy hug that sees you standing next to someone you care about with your arm firm but relaxed around their shoulder, and the all-encompassing 'gosh-I-have-missed-you-I-wish-we-saw-more-of-each-other' bear hug. Any hugs are good and some are wonderful. During my time at The Plaine I have enjoyed so many varieties, it's been splendid. But what holds a really special place in my heart are the hugs and interaction and giggles and playtime that I have been lucky enough to enjoy with some very special little people. Many families have stayed. The majority will be welcomed back and a few will not!

Watching family dynamics is fascinating and after many years in this business it's easy for me to spot the different 'types'. It's interesting to watch as I have friends from all walks of life from tree-hugging, sandals-wearing hippies to top execs who enjoy having a nanny, to a stay-at-home dad as well as working parents who manage without outside help. All varieties of parents have been welcomed at The Plaine.

There's the London set who come down to the West Country for a few days, and somehow forget to bring their nanny but remember to bring their iPad, laptop, phone and Gucci handbag; so instead of leaving the day-to-day tasks and the breakfast and discipline routines to someone else they find they have to actively engage with their own children. And the children find they have two parents who don't really know them. This normally results in thunderous looks and total bewilderment and associated screaming tantrums. And that's just the parents!

Then there are the yummy mummy/daddy set who have children called Tarquin-Jona-Sardinia or Cristobella or Arno-Zappa-Skye. These folks can often be heard saying "I think we need to talk through our options for your breakfast" or "How does lying on the floor screaming help you to release your inner anger?" They arrive with a myriad of gadgets and special allergen-free pillows and soya-lactose-free-freshly-weened-goat's milk to avoid all the perceived sensitivities that their kids have. Personally, I reckon a good old fashioned roll down the grassy hill, some mud pies and bottle of pop in the fresh air might serve these kids better, but then what do I know?

Finally there are the others, and luckily for me they have been the vast majority. These are those great people who had kids to enjoy them and to offer them love, care and discipline in equal measure. They come in all different varieties and shapes and sizes but they are all groovy to get to know. Many children won't hug upon arrival on meeting the crazy lady at the B&B. Can't blame them really. Many won't hug within a day, but with a little encouragement and usually a dose of silliness on my part they often hug when they leave.

It might take me bringing my 'dog' Eric to the dining room table (Eric is made of metal and has a nodding head and a tongue lolling out of his mouth!) or playing peek-a-boo several hundred times with a tea towel or even offering to crack an imaginary (or a real egg for the particularly tough crowd!) on Daddy's head. But they nearly all come round in the end.

I remember adopting a new strategy that worked well for a summer. My inspiration came from a superb British film starring Emma Thompson. *Nanny McPhee* is a family comedy movie about a fabulous wart-ridden, uni-browed nanny who comes and changes the lives of the children forever. I needed something as I had a family staying with me with a couple of slightly humourless, almost sad-looking chidlers. (Chidlers; the name given to small human beans by the Big Friendly Giant in the book *The BFG*, which by the way if you haven't read then please do… its great!) I needed to break through this sullenness/unhappiness/hostility and unleash their inner hugs and giggles as they were staying for a week and I couldn't bear the idea of a bunch of down-focused miserable-feeling children at breakfast each morning. So my plan was one of humour with physical signs to it and thus the wart growing began. I was my happy jolly self as the family came into the dining room for breakfast.

"Welcome to breakfast and we hope you have a joyful day full of merriment," I quipped.

Small, brooding faces was the response.

"We all need smiles and hugs for the day, don't we parents?" I said hoping for something from these children.

Nothing; not a flicker from the smalls but much applause from the parents and other guests. I then explained to the young'uns how I was very similar to Nanny McPhee and that if I didn't get my hug and smile quota the most horrid thing might happen, as it had before, and I might grow warts on my face. This of course was met with nonchalance and a heavy dose of disdain at my utter ridiculousness by the ever-so-grown-up six- and seven-year-olds. A challenge, I thought! So I went about breakfast and when the time came to bring their sausages and eggs and toast on the side and some marmalade-without-those-stringy-bits-in-it I had miraculously grown my first rather large wart on my left cheek. It was big and black and thoroughly offensive and the father of the family nearly choked on his coffee when he looked up. Of course he then smiled but the children were diligent in their dourness. They gawped and gaped and nudged each other but still no smiles. I of course made no reference to my new addition.

Through two rounds of toast, extra coffee and tea I added warts to the infestation on my face until finally, the biggest, blackest 'wart' of all manifested itself on my nose. My glasses fell off, I yelped and finally the children cracked up. And when they did it was grand: lots of giggles and pulling off of warts and can-I-try-it-on? It's amazing what some old currants and some cheap water-based glue can do. This lightness fuelled the breakfast for the following week and when they left, my hugs were those of legends.

Of course there are exceptions to the rules of loveliness and giggles and one family proved this point beyond belief. The parents seemed to think that the utterly feral behaviour of their offspring was acceptable. Now maybe it's just me. I don't have kids of my own and will not be giving birth to any and some have suggested that these facts prevent me from 'understanding' children. They don't. I do have beautiful and splendid step-children who I adore and I believe it takes a community to raise a child, so I will always try and do my bit to help and encourage those around me with 'chidlers' and to be the best godparent my five godchildren could wish for. This will involve hugs, kisses and massive amounts of playtime along with a healthy dose of discipline, rules and an explanation of boundaries along with respect for other people and their property.

Maybe I am indeed now a grumpy old woman who saves plastic carrier bags because they might be useful, puts the dishwater on the plants, thinks a cracking night is pizza and a movie, is more Saga than lager and who eats less but weighs more. Maybe, just maybe it's me, but on the occasion of 'The Incident', *I don't think so*!

I still believe that people are responsible for their actions and for those of the people they call their own. As usual I smiled and welcomed the entire *** family into my home and then watched in amazement as the children proceeded to run around, shout, jump on furniture and open all the doors, even those that were marked clearly with a 'Private' sign. Now I know what you are thinking: 'Well Steph, they are only little and can't read properly'. But seven and eleven is old enough to read *and* to know better *and* their parents were holding their hands! After seeing them upstairs to the large family room, I listened in agony to the howls and screams of ill-tempered tantrums and the stamping of feet that ensued. I hoped that all my other guests weren't being tortured by the unruly behaviour of a few, as after all it was me who was responsible for the congeniality of my own home and I was aware that it was up to me to keep peace in the house.

Later on that afternoon I went to drop off their milk, which had been chilling in the fridge. This is when 'The Incident' happened and my incredulity reached its peak. As I entered the room there, in front of my very eyes and the eyes of its mother who was sitting on the bed watching it, was one short person, about seven years of age happily writing with a large crayon on the wall!

Now you can call me old fashioned, you can call me fussy, you can tell me I could have seen the 'funny' side but writing on someone else's wall in someone else's home is *not* acceptable in my book; so I did what any other self-respecting person would do and rather loudly and with eyes on stalks stared at the small person and said exactly what came into my head; *"What In Heaven's Name Do You Think You Are Doing child?!!"*

Green
Dress

Henry Dog ...
who knew we would find
each other?!

A new friend Julianna on Samosir Island, Lake Toba,
North Sumatra

The Centurions hanging around at breakfast

One should always travel fully armed!

The lovely Bermuda Gentleman with his handsome Morris Minor

Proper use
for an oven

Bermuda beach

The beloved Plaine Bed & Breakfast

In yoga it's a Sun Salutation... in Laughtercise it's a
Fun Salutation... this one is Bermuda style!

Bermuda Longtail

The only way to be safe in a kitchen

Chintz and ruffles everywhere

Home of the Rhett Room, Stone Mountain

Trusthouse Forte Assistant Manager...
great Hair... oh the joy of the 80's

My dad's typewriter which inspired me to write

Now OK, it may have come out a little harshly, it may have been just a tad abrupt but they were after all staying in *my* home and writing on my wall. I stepped back and was met by a disdainful look of disapproval for raising my voice to their little princess.

"Elise-Clover really doesn't appreciate you raising your voice to her," I was told.

"And I don't appreciate you letting your little girl write on my walls," I retorted.

"But really, you must see that she was just expressing herself," came the calm reply. "It's just her 'artistic flair' and you really shouldn't be angry about it. After all it will probably come off."

Enough said…

I think I have painted the picture for you.

I don't think I need to say more.

Feral children + unthinking parents = nightmare in B&B land!

*

All I can say is thank goodness for all the fabulous parents whose children will always be welcome at the Plaine. The ones who take responsibility, the ones who indulge me when I want to enjoy some time with their little ones, the ones who love their children enough to give them manners and teach them respect for other people and animals. I am so grateful to be able to enjoy these hugs as they cost nothing but offer so much, and really can turn a slightly average day into something marvellous!

CHAPTER 10

The Magical Front Door

The joy of opening the front door of the Plaine and I presume any other B&B is that you never quite know who will be standing there. The guests will have made the reservation (most times!) and I make a point of getting first names to help them feel more welcome. I know roughly what the dynamic is, i.e. parents with smalls, older people requiring a specific ground floor room, couples who request a four-poster bedroom. But that's it! Rodney and Daphne could be English or Australian, James and Suzanna could be nineteen or ninety, Jans and Elke could be male or female, Mitch and Banele with the children could be gay or straight. And none of those things matter. What *does* matter is that they get the best welcome possible, so that they feel at home and comfortable right from the beginning. They must have the best version of me when I open the door.

And, as you can imagine, the Plaine has welcomed many guests during my custodianship. A rough estimate is about 7,000 over the nine years and that's quite a lot of smiles and welcomes and greetings to conjure up!

And I love it. The variety of guests has been staggering and each reservation comes with its individual challenges and foibles.

Bob and Eddi were an interesting couple. They had made their reservation as Lord and Lady Bantrum and had not given their first names. When they arrived I eagerly threw open the door to find a very sombre couple: him in brogues and corduroy elbow patches on his tweed jacket, and her firmly trussed up in a twin set and pearls. As usual Steph gushes forwards.

"Hello and welcome to The Plaine. Do come on in out of the rain and it's really lovely to meet you," I said with a jolly handshake.

Clearly not what Lord and Lady Bantrum were expecting.

"While you are filling out the registration form, would you like some tea and cake?" I offered.

Again I was given the Lord and Lady without first names on the form and with quite rare austerity.

Hummmmmm, I thought, *I am not going to be called Ms Hill for the next few days and these people are in my home so I would like them to treat me with a level of familiarity.*

So, on the second cup of Darjeeling and a nice comment about the cake, I plucked up courage.

"I would love you to call me Stephanie, what are your Christian names?"

They somewhat reticently proffered Robert and Edwina. Excellent.

Off we toddled to their room, they quietly thanked me and I went about my daily business.

Now fast forward to day four of their six-day visit and picture the scene in the Dungeon Bar of the olde worlde George Inn across the road from my house. The couple who arrived and gave the impression of impenetrable standoffishness are with me. In big, comfy chairs near a roaring fire. We are drunk! We have had dinner, drunk lots of bubbly and vino collapso, had a couple of ports each and have now decided to look at the standard of whiskies which are available on the top shelf. Bob (Robert) has his shirt sleeves rolled up and no sign of a tie, Eddi (Edwina) has tucked the hem of her long plaid skirt into the knicker leg because she doesn't want to fall up the stairs on the way to the bar again. Robert and Edwina, Lord and Lady Bantrum, are long gone and in their place Bob and Eddi, two of the nicest, kindest, most interesting people I could wish to meet. We have chatted and giggled and I now know that they are pretty skint as they had to sell the family home due to land tax issues. Who would have known?!

*

When Ronnie and Chris came to visit I was expecting a couple from Gillingham who were perhaps just touring round and thought our B&B looked lovely. (This assumption made as they had booked last minute and I thought Ronnie had a lovely light voice.) What I did not expect was a beautiful couple of males, both over six-feet tall with immaculate make-up, perfect manicures and manners that would have done the royal family proud! Slightly preening in front of every, and any, shiny surface, they were delighted and overwhelmed and did any manner of oohhhhs and arrrhhhs at what they called the 'simply adorable' room we had assigned them. This continued for their entire visit when they presented me with a miniature rose bush for the garden as a 'huge thank you' for the kindness and, in their words, 'inclusion' I had shown them.

Mel and Ian were all the way from South Africa and arrived with an expectation of B&Bs they had stayed in years before on trips. They expected, I learnt afterwards, a woman in her sixties with a curler at the front of her headscarf, a fag hanging out of one corner of her mouth, a 10pm curfew and a woe-betide-you-if-you-stay-out-any-later attitude, wearing a flowery apron. I offered my traditional welcome and when they got a big smile and their own key and no curfew, they went from being ever so slightly anxious to being the most effusive, engaging and entertaining folks. So much so that after their scheduled three-night stay, they telephoned with a question.

"Is there a chance of another week with you guys there please?" they asked.

"Yes and brilliant and you might have to have a night up in our apartment as we're fully booked but yes," I cried.

Their reasoning was that they had such an entertaining time and wanted to spend more time with us at the Plaine! This then extended itself even further with a reciprocal trip to South Africa which saw Miles and me being greeted at Johannesburg airport, whisked to our lovely wing of their new home, given the keys to the brand new Land Rover to use during our stay and a trip to Pilanesberg National Park and then being flown by Ian in a Cessna over the land surrounding Johannesburg. And all because of a smile, they said!

The Essex girls who turned up for a hen night were another unexpected (even though they had booked) joy. They had booked the whole house for a hen 'do' and had confirmed online. However, after they had called for the hundredth time about showers and towels and make-up remover and stretch limousine service (?) and could they bring their own cheese, I was distinctly apprehensive about how this would all work out. I need not have had the tiniest worry. These loud, jolly, heavily made-up, fake-tanned girls wearing more bling than Liberace on his birthday were some of the most courteous and friendly girls I have had the pleasure to meet. They left their Jimmy Choos at the door, asked permission to use the kitchen to make a cuppa, shouted to each other about what kinda knickers and thongs they each had on and generally gave the Plaine an air of conviviality and vibrancy that was tangible. I loved having them in the house, and again when they left all was immaculate, all the beds were stripped and linens folded, and a bottle of bubbly was left to say thanks!

*

Then there are the ones where I feel I should have known better, and when I am told of my error I feel distinctly ancient! Danny had booked two rooms. Danny and his girlfriend arrived and went to their room; then his friend James arrived and he and his wife went to their room. I didn't see them till the next morning. So there I am serving breakfast and as usual, part way through we get chatting.

"So what do you do for a living then lads?"

I am sure one of the girls smirked but I had no idea why.

James worked with filming he said, and out of interest I asked what.

"Oh I do some of the stuff on the Marvel films," he replied. OK, I thought, none the wiser.

"What do you do then, Danny?" was my innocent question to his mate.

"Oh I am a musician."

"That's nice," I replied. "Are you in a band?"

More sniggers from the girls.

"Um, yes, have you heard of McFly?"

Now even this dinosaur has heard of McFly. Couldn't name any of their songs, but I know the name. At this juncture it's important to point out that at the time I was step-mum (monster) to two teenage step-children who lived with us full time and two of my housekeeping helpers at the B&B are sixteen.

McFly, I thought!

Potential of brownie points with teenagers, I thought.

After checking with Danny that it was OK to do so, I rushed upstairs, gathered the assorted teenagers together and mentioned casually that Danny from McFly was downstairs. Hummmmm, there is a sound that would possibly make a dog's ears bleed and make paint peel. It is a sound probably audible in space. It is that distinctive thing called the teenybopper-squeal-of-glee and delight and almost hysteria that accompanies news that is pleasing to them. And that's exactly what I got! Lippy was quickly taken from bags and applied, hair was flicked one way and the other and even the boy teenager put on a clean shirt. (Had I known that was what it would take I would have lied and told him the whole band were downstairs weeks before.)

They primped and preened for a few minutes till I reminded them all that these guys would be checking out of the house soon, so they had better get a wiggle on to come and meet them. Danny was brilliant and had pictures taken with them all. James, it turns out, doesn't just 'do some stuff with the Marvel films', he is in fact one of the special effects professionals. This propelled him to God-like status for the teenage boy and by default for a few glorious heady moments I wasn't evil step-monster anymore, but instead the bringer of great things to my brilliant and thoroughly appreciative step-kids! Possibly the best moment of life in B&B land.

*

Preconceptions and prejudices have no place in B&B land and definitely no place at the front door. You simply NEVER know who will walk into your home and what they will bring with them. The thing that stands true for me through all the door-openings and greetings is that everyone I meet is simply a friend I haven't met before, and that is how they will be treated. The final truism is also that I have complete faith that the vast majority of people who come across that threshold are there to be kind and decent and generous of spirit and to be surrounded by that on a day-to-day basis is truly a blessing.

CHAPTER 11

The UN Should Eat Together

Looking back at the great variety of people who have been welcomed through the doors of the Plaine, it's truly gratifying to be reminded of all the nationalities and fascinating folk who have enjoyed (or endured) some good old-fashioned hospitality.

During my time in B&B land I met people from all walks and many languages of life. Some favourites include the quiet musical couple with the gentle Scottish lilt from Eriskay in the Outer Hebrides, for whom a trip to the South West of England was a true adventure of fifteen hours and nearly 600 miles. They wanted to come and experience the Bath Music Festival and the Plaine was their choice of destination.

Then there were two big strapping South Australian miners and their tiny wives. They had planned and saved for years to come to what they called their 'Motherland'.

"We wanna see where the rellies were from ya know," they told me whilst bashing their heads on a particularly low beam.

"Yeah, Margie's sister's nephew reckons they all came from St Philip's Norton so we're here to find 'em."

Steeped in history, the village of Norton St Philip does seem to offer some of the best information for people searching for their roots in the area. The church offers good records and the well-kept graveyard gives a place to 'meet' your relatives who have passed. I was really lucky to be offered an insight into the village early on in my tenure at the Plaine, when a friendly lady from the local WI came to visit. She epitomised the notion that many have of this organisation with her neat perm, beige ensemble and sensible brogues; she was intelligent, informative and very convivial. We had tea and cake and I explained my fascination and love of my new home. There was in existence, she explained, a series of folders which had been created over many years and which shared information on some of the local families in the village, along with photos and mementoes. This would offer an introduction for me and I would be welcome to see them. I was delighted that I should be seen fit to be the keeper of these historic volumes. They were intriguing to look through with references to some of the families who have roots back to Cromwellian days in Norton St Philip along with more recent pictures of children in front of my house who have grown up and now go drinking in the pub! This kind of nostalgia and preservation of history is so important, and being able to share that with my Ozzie visitors was exceptional.

Other visitors include a couple that played their rabab (Moroccan fiddles) at breakfast, bowing melodies that sounded like angel song. Several guests enjoyed a stand-up comedian who used his six-night stay to practise his new material on them. And we had a bunch of chaps who came to stay for a week as they were working on a shop installation in the nearby town. At over six-foot tall with bald heads and multitudinous tattoos, they looked the kind of people you really wouldn't want to meet on a dark night in a lonely alley but there they were, asking politely whether I could possibly make them toast soldiers to dunk in their lightly-boiled eggs, please and where could they leave their muddy boots.

Kiwis and South Africans came and congenially argued rugby and ostrich farming while bringing back memories of my travels to both countries, and a Ugandan family who were moving to the UK to escape horrors which are quite unimaginable to us brought me flowers from the hedgerow and taught me that 'Tradukka' and 'Amani' mean peace and love in Swahili. French people sat with Germans and Italians with Mexicans; Russians spoke slowly and congenially with Chinese and the Irish talked with the Israelis about the troubles in their countries. Croatians talked to Egyptians and the Norwegians laughed heartily with Brazilians. There really isn't any better sound than that of laughter and conversation resonating around your home, and to have that feeling each morning when you have introduced previous strangers to each other is truly magical.

As people come into the dining room at the Plaine I suggest where they might sit. Over time you get an inkling of how private people want to be or how gregarious they feel. To sit them on a small table might be appropriate, but more often than not there is a willingness to communicate with people from other lands, a willingness to share thoughts and ideas and a willingness to work through the boundaries of language to interact. Also, as I always say when checking people into the guesthouse, it's very old fashioned to sit at little tables and pretend that no one else is in the room. My idea of having bigger tables where people can mingle a little isn't new; it's what many cultures do. I simply do it British-style with toast racks and individual teapots.

And the stories and conversations you hear are always intriguing. While I was poaching and frying and grilling and toasting I could hear explanations gently conveyed in simple English; I heard debates on how to get the best from a ukulele and how to do traditional tongue and groove panelling. I heard enjoyment in sharing these experiences. I heard people simply being! They shared places where they had been and places they were going. People even car-pooled to a specific event when two hours before they hadn't known each other. People exchanged business cards with a view to communicating in the future, and in some cases people met up for coffee whilst visiting our nearby historic city of Bath. One day I had to physically shoo a group out of the dining room so that I could clear the tables! The group consisted of a musician from Sweden, a composer from London and a Peruvian singer, all of whom had been to a specific course on musicology and wanted to create a new and hopefully unique musical sound. They were so excited and wanted to create it there and then, to talk it through, get their instruments and simply get on with the creative process. So I did what I thought was right and told them to go to their rooms, brush their teeth, bring their instruments and meet back in the dining room in twenty minutes. Mother Hen eat your heart out. This gave me time to clean up, find some biscuits, make a flask of coffee for them and leave the room for the day to allow this new band of friends space to conjure up something lovely.

*

When people talk and laugh together like this, it really is one of the most special sounds in the world. And there are two things I know for sure. One is that language doesn't have to be a barrier to communication; the second is that laughter is the universal language and is the best connector of all. Over the years I have had surprisingly in-depth conversations with people without knowing one word of their language, or they of mine. I travelled to Thailand for the first time when I was just seventeen, a long time ago now! Travelling up to the northern provinces of this vibrant country was not without its challenges as *farangs* (the Thai word for European foreigners) were virtually unheard of, and white, female lone travellers a rarity indeed. I vividly remember being in Doi Mae

Salong, a remote village near Mae Sai that would be my jump-off point to get into restricted Burma. Also called Santi Khiri, this hilltop village was colonised in the 1940s by refugee soldiers who came from Burma but were originally part of the Chinese 93rd Division that fought against Mao Zedong. Even now there is a decidedly Chinese feel with teashops and slopes planted with the China tea, oolong, coffee and fruit trees. It was into one of these teashops that I wandered and found myself sitting opposite a lady of indeterminate age. I smiled as I was offered tea and some sort of cake that I had pointed at in the window. She smiled back. We then had a 'conversation' for about an hour with no knowledge of each other's language. I found out about her family with gestures and using fingers to count. We 'talked' about the natural beauty of the area and the fact that this particular teashop had been in her family for many years; she explained that the tea I should be drinking for my slightly upset tummy was one which she told her helper to create. We laughed like small girls and we hugged when it was time for me to leave. We had 'talked' without words of the same language and that has remained with me all my life as a profound reminder of how we *can* communicate if we truly want to.

*

During my time at the Plaine it occurred to me on many occasions that the UN could take a leaf out of this book. Part of their remit is to develop friendly relations among nations and promote respect for human rights. By simply putting different nations around a table and asking them to share the butter or the coffee it seems that we have the beginnings of better relations already. Perhaps if the UN shared instead of stigmatised, attempted to understand rather than condemn, well, just imagine what the world might look like. Imagine a world where people communicate even though they might not understand.

CHAPTER 12

Facing the Day

In all walks of life and in all the roles that we play, there will be times that are better than others. There are times when things are going swimmingly, the world is full of joy, prosperity and love and you think how lucky you are. And then there are the other days. The day my beloved dad became unwell. That was one of those days and I had to deal with it.

But before you turn away and stop reading, this isn't going to be a whimpering litany of woes: it is actually an expression of bravery and determination, not only by my father, but by all of those who work in the hospitality industry and who have to consistently put a brave face on things to deal with the public. It's about the strength of humanity in us all.

To begin, let me paint a picture of my dad. Remember if you will the movie Chicken Run; now picture the Colonel Rooster chap who was ex-army, you know, stood bolt upright at all times and fought in the war, and who was terribly, terribly stiff upper-lipped and down to earth and full of vim and vigour. Got it? Well… that's my dad.

He, at eighty years young, finally accepted that he might actually be going into middle age whilst remaining perfectly convinced that he is invincible and quite unable to be stopped in any way.

He has false teeth, a hearing aid, two gammy legs, both war wounds from running in army wear, and he has had half of his stomach taken away. He limps, bellows, and contends that no one enunciates correctly, which is why he doesn't understand them, and thinks that everyone on the road is a complete imbecile! He is a force to be reckoned with and has a brain the size of a planet.

He is my rock.

He is also apparently not infallible; well that's what the medics said when he was taken to the hospital with the heart 'murmur'.

"It wasn't a heart attack," said Dad. "Just a murmur and obviously nothing to worry about."

But the 'murmur' needed to be attended to, and on February 10th my father was wheeled away to have a triple bypass. I don't think I need to go any further with the horrors that play on your mind when a loved one is under the surgeon's knife; suffice to say that the worrying hours were spent mainly pacing.

Dad being Dad came out of the surgery very well. Yes, he had tubes and whistles and plates and attachments, but he was alive and that's all that mattered; and by virtue of the fact he had lived and, in his inimitable style, we were all convinced that the road to recovery was clear and straightforward, that Dad would be up and about in no time and driving in under the recommended six weeks. Heavens, this is Derek Hill after all and to wait is simply not his way.

All was going well for three days. The tubes were coming out, the tests were coming back with positive results; that was until a little bug called C-difficile decided to plague my dad with new horrors. Those of you who have witnessed the results of this infection will know the degradation that occurs when someone contracts it. They lose their appetite and concentration; they lose their pride when they become incontinent; their will to fight diminishes when they see no way through. They slowly begin to slip away in front of your eyes. And all the time, because I lived two hours' drive away and had a business to run, every day I needed to put on the face my public needed to see.

The show must go on; so you put on your performer's face and trundle down to offer witticisms over the bacon and eggs and the occasional funny story whilst passing the toast. You entertain and explain the sights and ask if everyone else is having fun and what else you can do to help make their stay better. And all the time inside you're jittery and anxious. You're terrified that the world that you know will suddenly come to an end and nothing will make any sense anymore. You're worried silly about your dear ol' dad.

*

But you do carry on and you do continue the day-to-day running of the business and you do provide the usual service to your guests. And, as always, in the world of craziness and mayhem and incredible suffering there is always something that makes you smile and remember to be grateful. I have been astounded at the kindnesses that have reduced me to tears. Now, tears weren't far away on some occasions I have to admit, but sometimes kindness comes from strangers who have no idea of your circumstances who seem to know intuitively when you need a lift. For me it was flowers from an eight-year-old boy. James and his parents were staying with us and he simply handed me the flowers from the hedgerow and said, "Because your eyes look sad, Miss Stephanie."

He had no idea what was happening but he intuitively knew and did something about it.

There were the wonderful comments about kindness and hospitality in the visitors' book at the B&B, when I actually thought I had been distant at best, and perhaps downright indifferent at worst. But I hadn't, and people had continued to love our home, our hospitality and our particular brand of banter!

Hugs came from many a guest during this time to say thanks for making their stay wonderful and a little girl quietly told her mum to tell me that I have a good spirit.

All these came when I was at my lowest and my most scared. But it's not just me that has ever, or who will ever, endure pain and despair while running a business. Anyone who has their own business does it. In the world of running your own bed and breakfast you can't pull a sickie knowing that someone else will cover for you; you don't get paid holidays to use up or compassionate leave to take. Instead you put on your shiny happy face for the crowd. For this reason I salute everyone on the front line of the self-employed hospitality industry. It's challenging to have the buck stop with you and rewarding in equal measures, but what's utterly astounding is that you *do* get through and you *do* have fulfilling interactions with people and they are empathetic and understanding when you share even a small portion of your circumstances. Human nature is a marvellous thing and in this line of work, whether it's at a good time or during a challenging time, you get to see it in all its glory and long may that continue.

My dad's recovery was slow and arduous but recover he did; he is once again in indomitable form, thanks in no small part to the fabulous team who are the British NHS.

CHAPTER 13

Teamwork

It's amazing what can get done when people actually work together, isn't it?

When you look at major league teams who train together, communicate with each other and have a common goal it's easy to see how a team effort works. All of them grafting towards a common purpose. I have always been impressed by how a group of humans can come together and make great things happen, whether it's in battle, in sport or with the deceptively simple organisation of a traditional English village fete.

Teamwork is a very gratifying place to be and I am indebted to the brilliant team that I had at The Plaine. Yes, it was only small, but it was a well-organised, happy, communicative group that made the workings of The Plaine seem effortless. And I have absolutely no idea what I would have done without them.

When Miles and I first bought The Plaine I knew it would be lots of hard work. Had I known it would be 24/7 and 365 days a year I might have thought more carefully, but I had fallen in love with the property and I was completely blind to reason! I knew that I needed to understand every nuance and every crevice to make it truly mine and that it would be down to me to decorate, dress, adjust, co-ordinate and beautify the house to make it a winning bed and breakfast. So how did I manage when I did all the cleaning in all the rooms and the gardening and the decorating and the laundry and the breakfasts? What did we do when we first got here? What did I do pre-team?

Well, my most enduring memories are of having my head down a toilet for the vast majority of most days. Oh yes, and of knowing the exact status of the laundry mountain and how long the washing and drying would take and timing it to perfection ready for the ironing fairy (me) to come along and make it presentable! Oh, and being able to tell you to the last mushroom what supplies we did and didn't have, the whereabouts of the best jumbo dishwasher detergent in the local wholesalers and how many loo rolls of four-ply or more was the optimum to have in the cupboard at any one time! Oh, the heady joys of B&B land!

*

In the early days of running the Plaine, Miles would return from his day job to me calling out, "Number 3 loo" or "Outside pruning Wysty" (the wisteria) and all he usually saw was my bum swishing backwards and forwards on the floor of the showers or leaning over making the beds or sweeping the leaves away outside the front door... again. Or sometimes he would come home to a real treat. Me sitting at the bottom of the stairs with a mop in one hand and a duster in the other, and a lovely stripey pinny on having totally lost the plot on where I was, what I was doing and, in many instances, why! The Plaine has nine bedrooms and six bathrooms. It has a huge kitchen and entrance hall as well as a thirty-foot-long dining room. It is on a main junction in the village and has dust from cars and trucks, sheep and tractors and horses and combine harvesters constantly coming through the windows. It's a sixteenth-century property and has lots of nooks and crannies and little spaces for dust bunnies to live. So it's a major task to keep up to date with upkeep.

So after a long six months of massive change and constant work, I decided that I needed a little help with the rooms. Breakfast and the care of guests was my domain but stripping beds, cleaning bathrooms, climbing the laundry mountain which was getting bigger and bigger as our business grew from strength to strength – they all needed assistance. So I put an advert out and along came Bernice. South African by origin, she was loud and chatty and quick and dependable and just the breath of fresh air that I needed. After being with us a couple of months she would often come downstairs muttering "That blummin' Doctor, he doesn't give me a minute."

Or "I don't know why they keep hiding things but it's not gonna work."

Or "Man this is a lekker job."

It turns out that 'lekker' means like, which is good! The Doctor was a spirit who bothered her in Room 2 and it was little blue goblins who inhabited the house who were hiding her cloths and mops from her. Who knew!?

After Bernice came a series of lovely ladies who helped me and without them the business would have eaten me alive. Jill lived in the village and had grown up knowing the Plaine. This petite, independent sixty-year-old remembered when the building contained two small houses and the smaller of the two was a pub. She can remember when her aunt lived in the tiny two-up two-down hostelry and had beer and cider barrels in the front window of what is now the hall of the main house. Jill describes how her aunt would "sit like royalty in her rocking chair in front of the fire and tell people what ale to help themselves to from the kegs".

Another of my 'girls', Janet, had been living in the USA for years and relocated to the village with her family. From the north of England, Janet was gentle, kind and sweet as well as being straight to the point and a spade was a spade not a shovel! I never crossed Janet, I wouldn't want to, she would have told me exactly where she stood with no nonsense – my kinda girl.

*

After a few years of running the Plaine it became clear that I needed to do other things outside the business and that extra help was needed. That same week I had a random phone call from a lady who was considering moving to the village and would like some information on how community-spirited Norton St Philip was and what she should know before buying a house there. So I was blunt. I told her the good, the bad and the ugly. Sometimes heavy trucks go thundering through this medieval village when they shouldn't; she could meet lots of people through either the school if she had little ones; the church if she was a religious person; the village Mead (a large green common land in the village which everyone uses for ball games, dog walking, picnics and general mayhem) or in the pub, my chosen haunt! As an aside, it was always interesting to me to see how people really did fit into these categories quite well. Many overlapped on one or two, and the sense of community in this lovely village was, and still is, quite startling. Sure, people know your business or *think* they know your business, and sure, people will be a little nosey sometimes, but they will also look out for each other.

One Christmas it was decided that we would have a huge great Christmas tree at the front of the house: large lights, big bows, huge baubles, the works! We attached it to railings and to the house and it was secured in a large stone-weighted stand. None of these measures prevented it from being battered by the winds, and one afternoon whilst no one was home the tree tore away from its anchors and by the time I returned, it would have been halfway down the steep hill with broken lights and baubles lost in transit.

But instead of that I returned home to find that neighbours had worked together to re-rope it and to hold it upright till more stones could be found to prevent it from toppling over completely. A very large stepladder had been employed, at great risk to the climber, to attach even more ropes and wires to secure this big tree. The Plaine is at the centre of Norton St Philip and so the tree would have been a major focal point, but no one *had* to help. No one was obliged to help. My super-duper neighbours did this to help out their neighbours, which to me is the type of kindness that is sorely lacking in many communities.

So I told this and other stories to the random lady on the phone and later that month, she phoned to tell me she had bought a house about fifty yards from mine! When you meet Chelle she just oozes loveliness. Petite and almost elfin, she is obviously amazingly competent so it wasn't long before we were discussing how she could be a manager and give some new life to the B&B. And she did. Chelle moved things from one place to another, introduced a swish of colour and transformed a room! She is an amazing interior designer (that's what she's doing now), but for eighteen months I was lucky enough to have her on board helping guests to create memories and experiences.

After Chelle left, the vibrant young Neen came to work with us and quickly showed herself to be a new shining star. At just nineteen, Neen was light-hearted, dedicated, animated and had the most warming smile for every guest. I have long known in this industry that you can teach people many things, but natural aptitude and having an attitude of genuine charm and welcome cannot be taught. When Neen opened the front door to guests I know that each and every one of them felt the radiance of her huge smile. She, like all my helpers, became not only people who worked with me but friends who I entrusted with the business which was my world.

*

Having such a great team around me also offered me an opportunity to get out and do something that had been bothering me for some time. I love to make people laugh and I love the idea of helping people through challenging times. I had seen a documentary about a chap who was working with a group dealing with depression. He was introducing Laughter Yoga as a tool to help energise this group. I was intrigued. I investigated and went to London to do a two-day training course with a lovely chap called Joe, who has now become a life-long friend and with whom I go to Glastonbury Festival every year to put on Laughter Workshops. The training was good but I wanted to understand more about how this could all work, so I checked with Neen who said of course, she could manage and I should absolutely get on a plane and head out to India for two months to learn from the creator of this Laughter Yoga, Dr Madan Kataria.

So I did. Bangalore for two weeks of intensive training and then a road trip to Ooty and third-class train travel to Kerala. These are all stories in their own right but the upshot of my India trip was that I had in-depth training with and worked alongside Dr Kataria to truly understand laughter as a therapeutic tool. We even offered laughter as a send-off to a friend at his funeral, a request made by him and his family before he died. I was hooked and came home renewed, invigorated and committed to bringing more laughter as an exercise to more people to help then through challenging times. I have now worked in the UK, India and Bermuda with teachers and executives, nurses and cancer patients, teenagers and government officials as well as those challenged with a life dealing with Alzheimer's. I have been able to share with them the wonders of laughter as an exercise to reduce stress and anxiety. We all know how vibrant we feel after a good belly laugh, so to be able to access those empowering endorphins and feel the benefits of the serotonin release without relying on jokes, comedy and humour is truly delightful.

My work with laughter is a delight. It was facilitated by knowing that my team at The Plaine were totally behind me. This, I am sure, cannot be said for many walks of life where people simply go to a place of employment. At The Plaine, a family was built and we took care of each other. I am very proud to have been a part of that process and I am honoured to have worked with such great gals.

*

We have had some hairy moments, some scary moments and some run-off-our-feet-oh-my-goodness moments. When someone stuck a coat-hanger down the loo on the second floor, left without telling us and the loo began to overflow it was a challenge. When the wedding group of nineteen guests' arrival was imminent and the water tank decided to stop refilling itself resulting in no water pressure in any of the taps, or when the guests arrived with not one child but four and we only had one room for them so needed to remove all the extra furniture and blow up extra air mattresses at 9pm, there were challenges.

But to counter these we have had some marvellous times too. When the bride and her entourage turned up very stressed and we managed to calm her down so much that she demanded we all go to her wedding. When the shy newly adopted little Romanian girl came to us with flowers for being such special ladies and when we sat down over a 'staff' Christmas lunch and reminisced about the year, these are times when my team became family and their contribution to my world will never be forgotten.

CHAPTER 14

The Great Commute

B&B land is the perfect place to work for those of us who hate the idea of commuting. When you live where you work and you work where you live, then the commute doesn't involve trains, planes and automobiles. Instead it was simply a gentle shuffle downstairs from my lovely airy apartment, past guest bedrooms through the hall and dining room to the inner sanctum of the kitchen. Now just as an aside, anyone who knows me knows that for me, the idea of a kitchen being any kind of sanctum is crazy. I don't cook. I never have and with any luck I will never have to burden myself with that particular skill. I love to eat and I mean love to eat! But the idea of sautéing and blanching and adding a hint of whimsical elderflower essence to add just that certain something to my truffle soufflé: no, not this girl! Don't get me wrong; I love people who cook. I especially love those who cook for me and those who make cooking into some kind of art form. But the only reason I have a kitchen is because it comes with most houses.

When I live alone I cook. Canned soups and ping ping (microwaving, for the uninitiated) are favourites, and that all-time culinary extravaganza, beans on toast. Well, if that's what you are after then I am your girl. Anything more than that or a roast dinner and it's over and out. Which is why the irony of my purchasing a B&B wasn't missed by my family. It went something like this:

"Hi Mum, I have bought a bed and breakfast in Somerset. It's just gorgeous and it's quirky and lovely and we are going to have such lovely people to stay and I am so excited."

Silence on the phone.

"It has wisteria on the front and it's in a lovely village."

Still silence.

"Mum? Are you still there?"

She has obviously been waiting for me to stop gushing and take a breath before gently uttering the words, "Yes that's lovely, darling, but have you remembered that you don't cook?"

Talk about bubble-bursting. I was crushed, aghast and ever so slightly worried. But like most things in life, when you put your mind to it you can do them, can't you? I didn't know I could jump out of airplanes, but I did. I didn't know that I could get a BA Honours degree at the age of thirty-six, but I did. And so it was that I learned cooking. Well, actually I learned to cook breakfast. Only breakfast, which is what friends get when they come for dinner, or lunch or indeed breakfast. It's the same thing I appreciate, but at least I cook it well! And now I can create a full English breakfast for up to twenty people without really batting an eyelid. It's more difficult when I only have a few guests in as I lose a bit of concentration on the job in hand and want to pick up power tools (my real forte) and build new shelves or start bathroom renovations, with the result being an ever so slightly charred brekky. Anyway back to commuting…

Commuting people share the horrors of how they have to be up before they go to bed to catch the perfect train that gets them in the office at the perfect time, after collecting their perfect cappuccino en route! Well, that's if they are having a good weekly commute. Then there are the others, the ones who have to get up before the sparrows, crawl along the little roads to get to the big roads to sit on the really big roads in the traffic that is all going to the same place because someone at some point said, 'Thou shalt all come into work at 9am and doest thine work then thou shalt proceed to the homeward journey at precisely 5pm after committing thineself to a daily grind…'

Or:

Those diligent folk who work away and leave their warm, cosy house on a bleak Sunday night to head to their digs for a week-long shift of work and playing billy-no-mates in the pub because they are away from family and friends.

Or:

There are the ones who rush, rush, rush at the last minute, getting onto a crowded train with lots of other crowded rushing people, none of whom would ever dream of actually making eye contact with anyone else. They get to work harassed, sweaty and altogether in a very bad state and think that this will set them up for a productive day in the office. It makes me exhausted just thinking about it!

Now don't get me wrong. Not all is sweetness and light in B&B land, I can assure you. Drudgery, thy name is routine for this particular wild child, and the idea of doing the same thing every day, and I mean *every d*ay, is soul destroying. I have never wanted a life of routine or a life where I can expect certain outcomes on certain days and have a schedule to keep to. Much more for me the devil-may-care combination of spontaneity and surprise. But with hindsight I can see the comfort of routine. I can understand the sense of security in knowing almost exactly what's going to happen at this time and on this day and it must in itself be quite liberating not to be worrying about certain aspects of life as they hold no choice for you. I can see how traditions and routines can actually enhance a life. My Indian friend, who has the charming name Shiny, once explained how arranged marriages offered a routine, a certain freedom in that way.

She explained, "I always knew I would be married to someone of my parents' choosing at the age of about twenty-one. Because of this I didn't worry about what I wore [although she always looks beautiful] and I didn't worry about boys or relationships or meeting someone. I didn't need to angst over what my marital life would hold as it was already pretty much mapped out for me in terms of marriage and potentially children."

Instead she was able to concentrate on her studies and earn herself high accolade in her workplace at a large pharmaceutical company in Kerala, India. Paradoxically, the security of that routine marriage gave her freedom, in a way.

*

B&B land has shortcomings along with huge bonuses. The four-wall syndrome, for instance, has affected and no doubt continues to haunt many in this line of work. Because of the need to check emails, change linens, organise staff, check in guests and constantly upgrade your guesthouse, the vast majority of your time is spent within four walls. Lovely walls. Walls you own. Nice, gentle, comfy walls, but four walls none the less. I know I have felt trapped and caged sometimes and have felt like a dog on an extendable leash when I leave the walls. I get so far from the house running errands, buying stock and food and cleaning products and zap, the leash says 'No, not so far or so fast, lady; you must return to your gilded cage'. I have also had times when just one more sausage could be the breaking point. Others have felt the same way.

Emma, a new fellow B&Ber came to my door one morning still wearing her pinny. I knew this was not a good sign. She had been in business for just eight months.

"Sugar prices are going up you know Steph," she mumbled. "And what about the farmers' market, they are crippling us with the lack of cherry tomatoes. And what is it about bloody Fairy soap that just makes me want to scream?"

She then proceeded to simply sit on the floor and weep. Not small, snivelling, girly whimpers either. These were huge, salt-laden, deep-rooted, sorrowful tears of despair. I was dumbfounded, so sat down on the floor next to her with tissues and empathy and a hug. After about ten minutes when the majority of the snot and tears had subsided, the reasons for her apparent meltdown came tumbling out in a torrent of words.

"Well, the bacon burnt and not just once nor twice but three times. And then I put it under the grill and it had burnt again. It was all too much and I am obviously not cut out for this business. I don't know why I thought that moving to the country and living in a lovely old house, with lovely horses and lovely fields all around us was such a smart idea. It was all simply madness and I must return immediately to my highly stressful corporate job in a law firm in the centre of Birmingham as I am clearly not cut out for country living."

She continued the woeful stream about guests with bad manners and people who didn't use the make-up wipes that she provided in the bathrooms so that she was left with smears of fluorescent orange foundation all over the sheets. This was followed by the wellies that were strewn over the kitchen by children coming home after an afternoon playing in muddy fields (you don't get that in Birmingham) and finally the smell of the bloody manure when it was being hauled by tractors through the medieval village in which she lived, to be used on the great open fields that surrounded her house! She even cried about the smell of freshly cut grass, the new lambs in the fields and the villagers who are all so bloody nice! It was at that point some twenty minutes and many hugs and tissue-drenchings later that she finally looked up at me. I of course had been through this particular sense of bewilderment earlier in my B&B career and had felt almost exactly those emotions. So when I looked at her and smiled slightly, she was quizzical.

"It's just that last week you were handed a Silver Award for Tourism for the most outstanding breakfast in a new B&B," I said. "And all your guests love you and those people booked a wedding with you last week too because they simply liked you. But, you are right," I continued, in a mock Shakespearean play-type way, "you must get to Birmingham quick, quick and harness yourself into that hamster wheel as quickly as possible, as you are obviously a complete failure! You must forsake all the great things around you and give in to the power of the burnt bacon. You have been beaten and will remain rubbish so must run away quickly."

She reached for another tissue and I think might have been contemplating another round of waterworks, but then she caught my eye. And I smiled. And she punched me on the arm, which hurt a bit. Then she looked at me again and found me smiling; then I giggled a little and before we knew it we were both rolling around on the kitchen floor holding our sides helpless with laughter. My lovely friend Emma had reached her low point and had done the best thing she could and come to me and cried. Self-employment can be likened sometimes to pushing water uphill. You want it to go in the right direction and it's sometimes blooming hard work!

*

But I might have missed out some of the other benefits of B&B land. Apart from meeting great people from all walks of life and exchanging banter and bullshit with them, there are many small things that I enjoyed at the Plaine. Having a huge dining room to accommodate friends and family is a delight. It is wonderful to have had so many family birthdays and Christmases and surprise parties to celebrate births and promotions. There is always food in the house! You can't run out of tea, coffee, milk or biscuits, which is grand for when people pop in. It was also lovely to be able to help small businesses in the area: the florist who I recommended for weddings, the therapist who came and offered in-room massages, and the limousine service who collected hen parties and deposited them back after a raucous night out. It was important to help all small business owners where I could.

But even with all of this I still found myself having a four-wall moment, which is why I decided after a few years of creating a new business model, working really hard to gain a good reputation for repeat business and having my dynamic team in place, I was able to go off to India (see Chapter 13 'Teamwork') to learn about Laughter Yoga. After becoming a certified Laughter Yoga leader I found I could do laughter workshops and sessions around breakfast, after emails and before check-ins and I found that sharing stories about laughter around the breakfast table gave me more impetus for my laughter sessions, as well as bringing even more silliness and entertainment to the tables in the dining room. A winning move all round which still didn't mean a long commute or an increase in routine, but did mean an increase in my involvement with humanity outside the four walls.

Self-employment isn't for everyone. It has its downsides.

I will never have a weekly pay cheque coming to me.

I don't have the luxury of holiday pay and bank holidays off.

I am absolutely certain that no one is going to offer me sick pay.

And sometimes my boss is a bitch, works me too hard and doesn't encourage me enough, but I can honestly say that its rewards far outweigh its negatives.

So for now, and I reckon forever, I will be one of the self-employed with no commute to commute.

Being in charge of your own destiny is what matters to me.

Oh, and after all these years of working for myself I might be completely unemployable!

CHAPTER 15

Festivals, Folk and Firearms

I know I have been exceptionally lucky to be able to live in the beautiful countryside of the South West of England, but little did I know that this luck would extend to being really close to lots of music festivals. And really good ones at that! Glastonbury is by far the best known. It is set in over 900 acres in the Vale of Avalon, an area steeped in symbolism, mythology and religious traditions. It encompasses just about every genre of music as well as welcoming men, women, children and the odd dog. But there's a whole bunch of smaller, more intimate festivals that have intriguing line-ups and really good vibes. The Llama Tree Gathering is folky, Bath Festival is posh and Frome festival is astonishing in its variety of performers in such a small venue. Having frequented many a festival (some slightly more dodgy than others!) in my time I was thrilled to hear that there would be one just down the road, quite literally one and a half miles away: the Trowbridge Pump Festival.

As soon as I heard, I put my ear to the ground in my usual eager-beaver style to contact the creator and operator of this gathering and enquire whether he might need some accommodation for his musicians. I turned up trumps and I was able to meet the legendary

Alan Briars, who was not only a celebrity in the music world but also one of the nicest people I have ever met. He had created the festival from nothing thirty years previously, and was now able to invite the likes of Chrissy Hind, The Levellers and *American Pie* Don McLean. Alan came to visit and in true rock 'n' roll style we had tea and cake and he booked the house for five nights, with the festival gang having the house to themselves. I was elated at having the house occupied for a week and all set to meet some truly excellent people into the bargain. *Wonderful,* I thought: *a house full of folky musicians singing gentle lyrics and perhaps enjoying a sip of ale!*

The reality was a little louder, a little less sombre (or sober) and a *lot* more muddy than I had predicted.

They rocked up to the front door covered to their knees in muddy boots with guitars and drums and tambourines and a ukulele, reeking of a local brew and weed, and proceeded to walk past me into the house as if they owned the place! *Hummmm,* I thought, *perhaps time for a chat.* So I mentioned a couple of things like congeniality and respect and where the heck was my ale? They dutifully hung their heads and muttered things like 'sorry' and 'won't do it again'. The smallest of these guys must have been six foot two, with long blond dreads curled up in a ponytail, wearing a replica American Civil War uniform jacket over a pink kilt and purple Doc Martens. I really didn't want to be the grown-up, but I really couldn't handle the idea of a wealth of festival mud (poo and pee enriched as it's held on a farm) to be trudged through my house. But it's at times like these that my inherent belief in human nature really comes to the fore. A little reminder note on the front door next day asking that boots be left in the hall saw these great beefy, punk-folk-hippy-rockers gently sitting down on the front doorstep ensuring that they, and everyone else who came to the house, not only removed their shoes but placed them carefully on old newspapers they brought themselves. They then all proceeded to gently wander through the house in their socks looking anxiously behind them for traces of mud!

Now, it might have been fear of the scary landlady that did it, but I think not. They, like all of us, need a gentle reminder to be aware of others and offer a little care when possible. It's not difficult is it? It's not difficult to offer praise, or thanks for a job well done or to compliment a random stranger. I believe that deep down people do genuinely care about each other and do genuinely want to be kind. And when you make the effort to make a difference for a random person, well, it feels really, really good.

*

Having a bed and breakfast means you meet lots of people lots of the time and its fun and entertaining to remember some of the lovely folk who have crossed the threshold of the Plaine. One really lovely lady turned up for a wedding that she was attending in a nearby village. Down she had come from the frosty North presuming that by the time she got to Bath, she would be in the balmy South West. She had been away for a few days and hadn't realised how cold the nights were. Breakfast came and she looked decidedly uneasy as she munched on scrambled eggs and lashings of toast and coffee. Anyone could tell, as she kept looking out of the window anxiously, that she was trying to figure out how she could wear her pyjama bottoms under a posh frock to keep herself warm. Little did she know, but help was at hand.

"What colour is your dress?" I asked. "And is the wedding in a field? And your shoes... they have heels?"

I could see her apprehension about being chilly.

So I did the only thing possible and ran upstairs to my cupboard, which houses the large, and some may say somewhat excessive, collection of pashminas and scarves that I have gathered from around the world over the years. I love them! You can wear them as a scarf or a shawl or a hoody or a skirt. They can be used to cover your shoulders in Indonesian temples where to expose them is not acceptable, or as a pillow on flights that allow you time to cuddle up in a window seat on your way to the next adventure.

Knowing her dress colour, I brought several pashminas downstairs and knocked on her door. We had a lovely time draping different ones over and round her until she had a mixture that accentuated her outfit, but also kept the South West wind away. She put her jaunty little (soon to be bedraggled) straw hat on and had the most delightful time, warm in pashminas that had travelled the world.

*

Some guests have brought great hilarity into the house when they didn't even mean too! On a blustery day in January, a couple came to the door and practically shunted me out of the way with a barrage of huffs and puffs and "Good days" and "You must be the proprietor" and "Where shall I stash my gun?"

To say I was a little taken aback is an understatement! *Mi casa es su casa*, absolutely, but really? Lord and Lady Fontborough had come down from London for a little shoot with a local lord and had decided to slum it with us. The others had stayed at the very distinguished (and very pricey) Babington House about three miles away. They 'wanted' to be closer to the action so had decided to stay with us. Having seen them arrive in a beaten-up old Rover (not even a Range Rover), their whole demeanour smelt a wee bit like bullshit to me, but OK, I would let them keep up their pretence of prosperity if that's what made them happy. It's sad when people feel the need to falsify themselves to increase what they perceive as their 'standing' in public. Genuine people in every level of society are far more interesting and engaging than anyone with a façade. I showed them to their room and they were very happy, but more curious about what time the George Inn across the road opened its doors so they could have some lunch. Not long afterwards I heard the front door close and that was the last I saw of them until breakfast.

We had some American guests staying with us and they were in the dining room for breakfast. Many of us have had the dubious pleasure of encountering some of the more boisterous and garish of our American cousins, who will tell you that the Thames is a trickle and that Buckingham Palace looks a lot like their summer place in Texas. (I am allowed to make generalisations; my Tennessee-born, Texas resident sister-in-law says so.) This couple, however, were completely the opposite. Polite, quiet and considerate, they enquired about the history of the village and we chatted happily about all things British. Everything in the dining room was serene until the Lord and Lady appeared. They practically fell through the double glass doors into the room and bumbled into their chairs, obviously still hammered from the night before. Bloodshot eyes, gravelly voices and that lovely odour of stale alcohol and cigar smoke that only comes after a major bender. Now don't get me wrong, benders are not exactly foreign to me, especially after moving to a village where there are two pubs within twenty-seven steps of your front door. I have enjoyed many a night's entertainment and entertaining, so I would never cast aspersions. I simply know the signs when I see or smell them!

This mad and lovely couple proceeded to regale us with the story of their shenanigans the day and night before. About them heading to the George for some 'lunch' and meeting some local people to chat with in the bar. (I knew exactly which locals they were and this Lord and Lady would have been a welcome audience to these Saturday afternoon ritual ale drinkers.) It would start innocently with some polite enquiry of their plans whilst staying in the village and knowing these two chaps, they would extol the virtues of me and the Plaine. Gradually as the hours of happy banter passed and the ale consumption increased the tales would get taller, the level of coherence would decline, with the result becoming a bunch of merry new best friends sharing life and love stories aplenty. I had witnessed this many times so I knew what had happened!

My Lord and Lady guests continued their story with a description of himself getting into the room and fumbling to make sure he knew where his gun was (under the bed apparently). Having found his weapon he proceeded to curl up on the floor, cradling said firearm and awoke in the same position in the morning. Then she shared an account that, despite her best efforts, entailed her being at the George for most, if not all of the day, and night! It went something like this:

"I left the George a little while after himself. He never could drink as much as me. [Obviously, but then a field of Young Farmers probably couldn't keep up with you either lady, I thought.] I got across the road and I knocked loudly on the window of the bedroom [luckily it was on the ground floor or else wisteria-climbing might have ensued] and I could see him on the floor with that soddin' gun but he wouldn't wake up, so I toddled over and slept on Roger's settee."

All of which could be believable had she not given me an overly covert wink, which suggested her sleeping arrangements might not have involved Roger's 'settee'.

And the noisy way these stories came out! We sometimes expect our American friends to have more energy when they speak and be enthusiastic in their volume, but I can honestly say that 'rambunctious' is not too big a word for this English couple. They were splendidly loud! The others in the room sat dumbfounded by the onslaught of sharing and then when the story of the evening was over, the Americans were bombarded by questions of what they thought of this country and would they like to go shooting? I think the grouse would have been quite safe from this pair of guns, as focusing on putting jam on their bread was enough of an effort. They brought a different dimension to an otherwise quiet dining room.

CHAPTER 16

Green Dress

From my earliest memories, I have wanted my very own proper fairy dress. Not the one that had to be put back in the dressing-up box at school. Not the one that Nina White had and kindly let me wear. One of my very own! The hand-me-downs from three big brothers suited my tomboy temperament but my inner princess desired one frilly, floaty, dress-up dress. A fairy dress from one of my brothers was improbable! But when I was six my mum bought me a yellow party dress with multiple petticoats and a big bow at the back. This was close to a fairy dress.

I loved that pale lemon bundle of prettiness and would have worn it constantly and possibly slept in it if allowed. I, like many girls my age, was in a Girl Scout Brownie group and with Christmas came the fancy dress party.

"Can I be a fairy, Mum?" little me asked.

"Ask your brother to help, he's the creative one," she replied.

So, out came the lemon dress and my middle big brother, Clive, became my hero by creating a huge cardboard and tin foil key, which would be attached to my back using silver string. This, with freshly shined black patent shoes, crisp white socks and rosy-red circles on my cheeks, created the illusion of a clockwork doll.

I won the prize. I was elated. The next year, whilst my beloved yellow dress still fitted me, Clive dressed me up with magical, big, floaty fairy wings and a wand. I was in heaven. My love affair with a fairy dress had begun.

*

Many years later in Brighton Miles and I were walking along the Lanes, which is the magically eclectic shopping area of this seaside town. I saw a stunning green fairy dress in a shop window. It was the green that you see in springtime when all the leaves are starting to come out and they have a light, emerald vibrancy about them. It was bright and floaty and had a layered, pointy-edged net skirt, with a tinkly bell on the end of each of its layers. It had a green satin bodice, spaghetti shoulder straps with ruffles, and on the back were the perfectly sized green wings which had enough wire to make them real without being too heavy-looking (I have studied wings). It was perfect.

Of course, it was in a small person size, but I decided to wander in and see if they knew where I could procure said item in my size. I couldn't believe my ears when I was told by the tattooed, pierced, shaven-headed, six-foot Goth assistant called April that, "Yes indeed we do have that dress. And yes, we do have it big people sizes. We have one in the back storeroom. Would you like to try it on?"

The cry of "Yes" could probably have been heard all the way to London! Ten minutes later and some cash exchanged, I skipped from the shop delighted beyond words.

Gleeful is an underused word but it describes exactly that heady-giddy-grinning-from-ear-to-ear feeling I had as I glided from the shop with my new dress in hand. Miles was a little befuddled by this exuberance.

"A green fairy dress? When will you wear this item of clothing? Sainsbury's shopping? The pub?"

Little did he know that nothing could calm my excitement and from that day, I have worn my green fairy dress at any given, some ungiven and some mildly inappropriate moments!

I wore it at our first New Year's Eve party at the Plaine. I invited friends and family and told them that it would be a green-themed dress-up party and that we would start in the house with drinks and nibbles, and then proceed to the Fleur De Lys hostelry across the road to join the village and the merriment and general madness of this time of year. My gang of mates dutifully turned up in a variety of outfits from jade to lime to emerald and we made a very eye-catching crew! The previous owners of the B&B had been somewhat staid in their manner and I think many people thought that the new folk who would own this grand house in the middle of the village would be sensible, grown up and congenial, but not rambunctious… oops! We rocked up, about ten of us, all in green, all slightly tipsy and all up for a jolly good time. Of course it had to be the first outing for my precious green fairy dress, which I topped with green eye-shadow, a tiara and fourteen-eyelet black patent Doc Marten boots.

We had a marvellous time and even the most conservative villagers recognised that, although I was just a wee bit eccentric, I was harmless and simply wanted to fit into this lovely village. I was delighted to be there with friends and family and I have been reminded of the green dress episode on many occasions.

That fairy dress represents more than just a silly outfit for me. It reminds me to be a kid: to be a little off the wall and to live life to the full. That green fairy dress also holds the most wondrous memory because of a very special lady who came to stay.

*

I got a phone call on an average Wednesday in May asking if I had three rooms for a weekend early the following month. Diary checked, I reported yes and took the details from Sheila for herself and her husband in one room, her parents in another and her brother and his wife in the third. Nothing unusual and nothing to make the reservation stand out.

The date came around and the brother Craig checked in mid-afternoon. At the Plaine we often have wedding, birthday, anniversary groups and so I enquired about the reason for their visit to us. The question wasn't unusual, although the answer was.

"Actually," said Craig, "we *are* here for a special occasion. My mum Jean has just been diagnosed with inoperable, terminal cancer. She has been given weeks rather than months to live so we decided to come away together to make a lovely lasting memory before the inevitable."

I have greeted many guests in my time but never been given that reason or indeed anything close to it. Yes, people have come to stay to attend a funeral but never (as far as I know) to create memories with a loved one with this kind of finite time frame. It was time for me to step up a gear and give my all to these lovely folk who were about to lose their mum. I saw Craig and his wife Jill to their room and rushed downstairs to the kitchen.

There's always a bottle of bubbly in my fridge so I put it on ice, took the champagne glasses up to our sunny patio and arranged cushions on the chairs to welcome the other members of this party. Craig and Jill were in on the ruse with me, so when Jean and Bob arrived with their daughter Sheila and son-in-law James, they were all whisked outside to enjoy bubbly and sunshine and the beginning of what I was determined to help make an outstanding stay.

Breakfast the next day was the usual assortment of mayhem and frivolity. We had a full house, which means two large tables and usually some good banter. This morning was no different and the other guests with small children shared stories and laughter while Jean's family joined in and told us of their plans to go to

Bath then onto the George Inn across the road for supper. As usual we got talking about how long I had been at the Plaine and where I had been before, and after telling them of times overseas, I shared some tales of life in B&B land.

I started to tell Jean the story of the New Year's Eve party and about how people had reacted to this green fairy nutter who was new to the village rocking up to the pub in her bovver boots and tiara. It was all fun and playfulness, so I asked her to have another cuppa while I popped upstairs. I wanted to show her something. Now, anyone who knows me will tell you that I will do most things for a laugh. It's the very best sound in the world to me so if you are laughing *at* me or *with* me, it doesn't really bother me. It's the laughter that matters.

So I ran upstairs, popped on the green fairy dress, replaced the seemingly now ever-present kitchen pinny on top, and came downstairs. It worked a treat and as I pranced and pirouetted around the dining room I heard applause and laughter and giggles. Just as I had hoped. Sheila went to her room to get the camera. Jean was enamoured with the frock and I had one more idea up my sleeve.

As I was acting the fool and showing her how much room there was for cleavage and expanding waistline when I went to the pub I suggested that as one size fits all, she have a little try-on. Reticent at first but then goaded on by the others, Jean gave in and followed me to her room.

"It'll never fit," cried Jean.

"Let's try," I replied.

Suddenly this beautiful, petite lady was wearing the magical green fairy dress and she positively glowed when she went back into the dining room to show it off. I was delighted. She danced with me in front of the fireplace; we had silly photos of us and the whole family with Jean in the centre with her fairy dress ensemble. It was a delightful start to the day and everyone left for their adventures with smiles and giggles and happy hearts, as well as happy tummies.

During the weekend many pleasant memories were made, photos taken and much laughter was had. I had arranged a nice table and fresh flowers at the George and had joined the family for a pre-dinner drink. We shared silly stories. Jean talked about times when her kids Craig and Sheila were little and how special they were to her. She told me how she and Bob had met at a dance and that she had been too shy to even look at him until he asked her to dance and then it was love at first sight. They had been married for fifty-seven years and they still held hands.

When Sunday morning came and we all said goodbye, we hugged and giggled whilst reminiscing about a special couple of days which weren't just beds and a bit o' brekky but were bubbly and joyful, enjoying spending time and creating memories with this special family. It was bitter-sweet for me as I hugged this demure lady goodbye. I hoped remission would prevail. I hoped the cancer would leave her.

Three months later I got another phone call. It might even have been on a Wednesday. Sheila would like to book three rooms please, but could Dad go into a different room than the one he had shared with his bride Jean on their last visit. Sheila told me they were bringing Jean's ashes back to scatter around the local area where so many cherished memories had been made. She told me that every day since their first visit to me Jean had told people about the girl at the Plaine and the lovely green fairy dress.

Words don't describe how that makes me feel.

Making a difference in people's lives can be so easy. A compliment. A smile. A hug.

CHAPTER 17

Jane Came to Stay

As I waited to collect Jane from the train station in Bath, I really didn't have a clue about what to expect. I had agreed to collect this guest at her brother's request. Charles had phoned me and asked if his sister could come and stay with me at The Plaine on May 23. I checked the diary and yes, that wouldn't be a problem; I presumed that it would be a one- or perhaps two-night stay. When he asked if she could stay for twenty-three days I nearly fell off my chair. A reservation of that length had never happened before and I was delighted, to say the least. Charles and I chatted about Jane and what she would need. He explained that she was coming home to the UK after a lifetime in Canada and that she wanted to see the old country. She was seventy-seven and travelling alone in a strange country, so I offered to collect her at the station. A single lady traveller appeared and looked somewhat disconcerted, so I approached tentatively.

"Is your name Jane and are you meeting Stephanie?" I enquired.

She was slim, white haired and really tiny, even delicate. She wore petite red patent leather shoes over white knee-length socks and a red patterned skirt with a blue woolly jumper and beige mac over it all. Her tartan headscarf was pulled down tightly to protect her from our crisp May weather. All her clothes seemed to swamp her and she seemed a little bewildered by everything, but then that's understandable for a lady who had left the UK in 1951 as a war bride and spent the majority of her adult life in Canada. It was the first time she had revisited her birthplace and clearly it was a very emotional return. I was glad to be able to try to make it easier for her.

We all know what it's like to leave someone or somewhere you care about, whether it is for a day, a week or a year. It's one of the massive challenges I face as I fulfil the wanderlust that has been my companion since I was seventeen and I first got on a plane to Thailand. I will never forget the look on my poor mum's face when she put her only girl, her youngest child, onto a Boeing 747 with an old, beige, scouts' 'A' frame backpack and a paper ticket bound for the exotic Asian destination formerly known as Siam. It must have been nerve-wracking for her, but boy-oh-boy it was a whirlwind for me. I had once been on a plane with my parents to visit family and friends in the USA. But this was altogether different. I was seventeen. And a girl. And alone. There was no internet and no mobile phones to chat to people whilst travelling, and the world felt a lot 'bigger' then with international travel for teenagers relatively scarce. I had booked the cheapest ticket, which in those days, meant flying through various countries to get to my final destination. I flew from London Heathrow to Bulgaria then to Dubai and finally into Bangkok.

Bulgaria was cold, really cold, and not much heating in the vast, barren, brightly lit airport that sported only one venue for something to eat. The menu consisted of homemade rakia (Bulgarian brandy), Coca Cola and hotdogs. There was a random and eclectic mixture of passengers variously sitting around on the few plastic chairs that were available or lolling against walls drinking or trying to sleep on the cold marble floors. There was also a group of Jamaican athletes who had brought a boombox. (It's circa 1982 so boomboxes were cool.) They had reggae, they had rum and they were gonna have a good time no matter what. And it seemed rude not to join them as they bounced, danced, and bumped the beats from Mr Marley through the entire Bulgarian airport. We only had a three-hour layover, but by the time we left that airport I had made friends, laughed and danced and got quite tipsy on lots of rakia, which I later found out was 77 per cent proof. It was during the next flight to Dubai that I started to regret my gyrating interlude as the hangover kicked in, hunger repositioned itself in my tummy and I realised that I still had a four-and-a-half hour flight to Dubai, then another six hours to Bangkok.

Dubai is a beautiful airport and the sheer magnitude of the space was stunning. It had a central atrium, off which several concourses took passengers into different areas and terminals for flights to every corner of the world. I looked down into the atrium and was really impressed, although, due to the rakia interval, a little squeamish about the height. I found my gate and waited for what seemed like ages until a chap came and sat next to me dressed in a pilot's uniform. We started chatting in pigeon English/Thai and I learnt that he was actually the pilot of the plane to Thailand but that he had been told to wait until more checks had been carried out on the aircraft before he could board again. *Well,* I thought, *at least if I have the pilot then the plane can't go without me.*

And it didn't. But it did get delayed by about five hours. I was tired, it was warm, and the rakia was still coursing through my veins. I woke up with a start, looked up and found myself nuzzled into the crisp, white uniform of the polite (he didn't shove me off his shoulder when I went to slumber) young Thai pilot. I must have drooled. Perhaps snored. Great first impression of your country to the outside world on your first real adventure alone. I did finally get on the plane to Thailand and arrived safely to enjoy a few months wandering the South East Asian continent. But leaving those you love is never easy, and so being able to offer some comfort and camaraderie to Jane was important to me.

*

Jane ensconced in the car, we got back to The Plaine and I settled her in. The following days were lovely. She didn't want to 'do' anything in particular; she just wanted to 'be', so I simply included her in things I was doing. Jane and I did grocery shopping together and she marvelled at the new buildings and bigger roads compared with the ones she had in her memory of fifty-seven years before. We walked and talked and shared stories of her world and mine. Jane was very innocent in many ways and had led what seemed a very happy and sheltered life in Canada.

This became even more apparent one morning when we got into a conversation about plumbing. It was a Sunday morning and the previous day, an attractive if slightly ditsy thirty-something blonde had checked into the room next to Jane's. Their bed headboards were on opposite sides of the adjoining wall in separate rooms. The walls are thick in many areas of the house and not so thick in others; so, although you couldn't hear what was being said in each room, it was inevitable that you would be able to hear some noise if it was loud enough. So the blonde, who will now be known as Barbie Doris, was going off to a wedding.

"I might not be home till late," she said.

"No bother, just remember to take your key!"

Off she went.

Jane and I had a nice evening and went to bed around 11pm. At 2.30am, I, and I suspect the entire house and much of the village, were woken by the shrill continual ringing of the front doorbell. Not just a little apologetic touch of the bell but a drunken leaning onto the bell-because-my-finger-is stuck-to-it-and-I-am-too-sozzled-to-move-it kind of ring. Now, as you can imagine at 2.30am, there had better be a fire, an emergency or a winning lottery ticket to justify making that kind of a din. It turned out to be none of the above but simply an ever-so-slightly hammered Barbie Doris dragging along a 'new friend' to stay the night.

It was Miles who went and opened the door in a state of some agitation and in a rather becoming fluffy white dressing gown, which was the first thing to hand!

"Forgotten me key," slurred Barbie Doris.

"Which room are you in?" enquired Miles in his usual personable way.

"We're in 4," said Barbie and hauled her new friend inside.

Miles didn't know she had only booked a single occupancy room so left them to it and returned to bed.

Next morning, about an hour after breakfast had been cleared away and most guests had left, Barbie Doris's 'friend' came ambling downstairs. Dishevelled and reeking of whatever cheap aftershave he had on the night before along with a dose of whiskey and cigarette allure, he came in.

"Any chance of a late brekky please?" he inquired.

Cheap aftershave boy got 'the look'. For some people it's one used for your offspring that tells them they are right at the end of your limits and dire consequences will occur if the 'look' is not heeded. (My mum can still conjure up that look and she is ninety-one!) For other people, it's a look of derision and disdain that can wither the strongest will and make a kitten from a lion. My look said something along the lines of who-the-heck-do-you-think-you-are-daring-to-come-and-demand-breakfast-when-you-weren't-even-due-to-be-staying-here. It was maybe a wee bit harsh, but interrupted sleep and disrespect will do that to me. He was last seen trundling sheepishly upstairs, getting Barbie Doris and heading out.

Tea and toast and calm later on, Jane approached me with a strange look in her eye.

"Steph, do you have ghosts in the house?"

"Well there are all sorts of strange sounds that occur, Jane. What makes you ask?" I said, not wanting to freak her out by saying that yes, there are lots of spirits in my house, but I don't want you to be scared.

"Well," she said, "last night at about three o'clock there was this really strange knocking sound and it was quite repetitious. It seemed to be coming from right behind my bed and then there was a sort of quiet wailing that accompanied it."

She waited for my response, which I was trying desperately to find without offering her an insight into the true origins of the 'knocking'.

"It didn't stop for quite some time, so I wondered whether it was a ghost?"

I had to keep my face straight as a realised what dear, sweet Jane had experienced. I suggested that it might have been the plumbing or a dream, as I didn't think the ghosts would be making that kind of noise at that time of night. I didn't have the heart to tell her that the only spirits on that occasion were those consumed by Barbie Doris and her 'friend', and that the repetitious banging might have been something to do with their drunken shenanigans.

CHAPTER 18

The Horror of the Silent Breakfast!

The word 'breakfast' is derived from the phrase 'breaking the fast'. We fast while we sleep, so breaking that fast means we have lived through the night, thus breakfast should be a celebration and the most joyful meal of the day. Breakfast for me is an opportunity for a new beginning that sets the table and therefore sets the tone for the day! And it's really one of the only 'touch points' (in customer-care speak) where I can make an impact and make a difference to someone's day. Bed and breakfast means exactly that: people come and sleep and they eat breakfast and then they leave to go off and have their day or go onto their next destination. So breakfast needs to be the best I can provide and I have always believed that the food, while not secondary to the experience, is only a component of it. You can have a bottle of Cristal champagne and fresh quails' eggs marinated in the coal sheds of a Peruvian monk, but if you are sitting in an unwelcoming atmosphere and no one smiles around you then it's simply not going to be enjoyable. OK, I take back the bit about the Cristal; I could eat just about anything anywhere with a bottle of this particular tipple.

At the Plaine we offered a hearty breakfast, which I am proud of. Fresh yoghurts, local seasonal fruit and a selection of lovely cereals made our breakfast buffet a great start and the traditional offerings for your 'main' breakfast could be ordered from our menu, ensuring you have what you want on your plate and nothing else. No, we didn't offer pancakes (American), croissants (French), or congee and noodles (Chinese). But we did offer a whopping great traditional English breakfast along with the options of organic gluten-free bread and soya milk as I know first-hand how allergies and food intolerances can negatively affect your life. Isn't it funny, though, that when someone finds they have one allergy it seems to create a whole lot of other 'conditions' that they didn't know they had. I even gave in and bought small plates and cutlery with a famous mouse on them, high chairs and booster seats for our small visitors and created menu translations for those who arrived without knowing what to expect.

However, the main thing that we offered at the start of every new day was a congenial atmosphere in pleasant surroundings and a hearty meal to get people off on the right foot.

The setting for this meal is a large, open dining room with funky off-centre windows that have creaked and slanted with the movement of the house over its 400-year history. The beams are low, the walls are three-feet thick, the artwork eclectic and the furniture a mad mixture of many styles cobbled together over the years. It's warm and inviting and everyone says they love this room.

What we also offered was a warm welcome, a happy disposition and the desire to help make the day brilliant. Which is why we offered guests the opportunity to sit at large tables instead of little individual impersonal tables and the opportunity to meet new people should they choose to. No, it's not everyone's cup of tea, and it was interesting to learn how to spot who should sit with who when checking guests in. If people had children they could sit together or if there were grandparents without children we knew they would be more indulgent of a baby than a young couple on a romantic weekend. It got quite easy to recognise which guests to sit together and we always had a small table to use in case we recognised a real desire to be alone at breakfast.

So, although congeniality was at the top of the breakfast priorities at the Plaine, it was inevitable that on one occasion this particular brand of hospitality didn't work out. Usually you will get a mixture of folk. Some people show up with their heads low, shoulders hunched wanting to make themselves invisible and eyes averted. Every bit of their body language conveys the message 'It is morning and I don't want to chat to people and you would be best served simply leaving me alone until cup three of my coffee addiction, thank you.' There are the Oh-So-Jolly Clan who are on holiday, have a sunny disposition and are keen to embrace each moment. They arrive right on time for breakfast with an attitude of 'Wow how lovely to meet new people' and an eager Labradorish quality which is both endearing and exhausting. They want to know your whole life story, how you got to the B&B, and how long you will stay and where were you before and and and... They will chat with everyone with open smiles and shiny eyes and are a joy to have in the room. Then there are the very quintessential vacationers who are thoroughly polite, will chat nicely to anyone in the vicinity, but need nothing more than their own company. They are neither aloof nor engaged. They simply are.

I loved listening to different languages, accents and points of view, and have watched new friendships grow. All manner of topics have been discussed ranging from vegan cooking to bull-fighting and from firstborn care to spotting the first signs of Alzheimer's and everything in between. The buzz of the breakfast tables is more often than not laden with a healthy dollop of laughter which I am usually part of, either as the instigator or the butt of jokes. It's gratifying when everyone is getting along and chatting... no silence!

But there was the one time… the time of the silent breakfast. Not just quiet; silent.

*

As usual, although I didn't particularly enjoy the cooking, I was looking forward to another banter-laden breakfast. There was always something good to listen to or share with others. I should have known when I opened the fridge and the milk jug had fallen over, thus covering nine-tenths of the contents of the fridge, that this would perhaps be a challenging day. I should have seen it coming when the oven did one of its little tricks and decided that 85 degrees wasn't the temperature to keep plates warm but that 180 degrees would be more appropriate and just about fried the glaze off the crockery. And when the doorbell rang with a delivery for the nice people next door and needed to be taken into a back room as it couldn't stay in the hall, thus making me forget about the bacon and ruining a whole grill tray… well, it should have been a sign to simply go back to bed and reboot! Little did I know that I would end up running around trying to make brekky and be efficient whilst also labouring to get people to feel comfortable and at ease in my home.

And so this day was one of 'those'.

My lovely guests arrived and sat down at the tables. As usual I introduced the cereals and yoghurt and explained with a wave of both arms in the general direction of the kitchen that this was where the main breakfast would be created and it would miraculously appear before their very eyes. On previous occasions this was met with a little smirk or a giggle or good old-fashioned laughter. But not on the day of the SB (Silent Breakfast). No, on this day it was met with stony stares of incomprehension. Every one of the guests was from the UK so I saw no reason for a language barrier, yet I didn't seem to be connecting with anyone. The next couple came in.

"Morning!" I gushed.

"Mornin'," they mumbled under thick sweatshirts and gruff exteriors.

No engagement and literally nothing in their body language to suggest that they thought I was even a tad amusing, even a wee bit whimsical. In fact to the contrary, they were now starting to look at me like I was barking mad.

But it didn't end there. Oh no. I had to keep on trying to make it better so found myself coming up with all sorts of inane comments in an attempt to engage with people and, because I was nervous, none of them rang true and I ended up laughing stupidly and rushing back into the kitchen. I told funny stories that weren't. I gave little anecdotes about the village that sounded hollow.

I burnt the toast…

I dropped the eggs and got orders wrong.

I made a complete fool of myself.

And I couldn't even make the radio work to bring a little musical distraction to the proceedings.

Argghh. There was this silence at the table despite my best efforts and I presumed that everyone was feeling awkward and that they weren't having a good time and therefore I was a rubbish landlady and shouldn't be in this business at all and might as well sell the place tomorrow.

And then… after what felt like hours of no communication and many moons of me angsting about how to rectify this deplorable situation, they finally starting talking about my antique brass bed warmer that hangs on the wall in the dining room. And then they were off. Discussions of its heritage, its uses, its authenticity (cheeky buggers!)… no silences, no awkwardness, nope; these lovely guests all had a jolly good natter about 'stuff' and had a giggle and shared stories just like so many other people had done round these tables on previous occasions. They ate, they drank, then off they all went on their merry ways into another day of vacation.

Meanwhile, I sat down completely knackered and bemused and befuddled. I had tried so hard.

I had made such an effort.

And perhaps that's exactly the lesson I needed to learn. Less is more sometimes and people need to find their own way, don't they?

Silence has its place and is vastly underrated in the world I know, but on this particular day I felt inept and at a loss to provide the most essential ingredient of conviviality to my guests. What I could have learned that day though was that sometimes you simply just have to give people space and that no amount of cajoling or attempts to interact will get people talking. Sometimes silence is where people are happiest. Lao Tzu, the philosopher of ancient China, once said that 'Silence is a source of great strength'. I think he is right and I think in the madness and mayhem of life, we can all find solace when we quiet our minds and find our own silence.

I didn't think this on a particularly nerve-wracking day at The Plaine, but I have done since!

CHAPTER 19

Bedspreads, Orangutans, Swedes and Handcuffs

Each room at the Plaine was individually decorated. Each had a big comfy bed, striking artwork and cushions to enhance the décor. Each looked distinctly different from the others. I was determined when I redecorated the whole house that each room should have a unique feel so that people could choose their favourite rooms in which to feel at home and relaxed. I have lived in many, many places in many countries and I know how important it is to feel 'at home' as well as secure.

No matter where I am I always seem to make a 'home' quite quickly. During the first month of a six-month walk-about in South East Asia I was in an outdoor street market in Yogyakarta, Indonesia and saw the most wonderful bedspread. It was made up of hundreds if not thousands of tiny triangles of material in tie-dye and batik and solid silks, all hand-sewn together. It measured eight-feet square. It simply had to be mine! I didn't really want to barter with the stallholder as I so desperately 'needed' this thing of beauty, but I knew better than to deprive him of this puzzling human need to haggle.

"How much is this please?" I asked.

"Three thousand Baht," he calmly replied.

Shock and horror. "No, no," I exclaimed and went to walk away, as is the tradition.

"OK, OK, special price for you lady. Two thousand Baht but only for you."

"How much? Are you crazy?" and so the dance begins in earnest. It's a little like flirting with raised eyebrows, hidden smiles and bodily gestures of horror and amazement. As I go to walk away, my new friend calls me back to him. It's interesting in Asian countries that, whereas in the West we gesture with an outstretched arm and the hand facing upwards in a movement towards our body, Asians put their hand facing down and appear to be trying to scoop you towards them. This is a cultural difference that many travellers to the East should be aware of. In many Eastern countries, to use your open palm to gesticulate is a sign of rudeness and when you go into a temple in the East you should never sit with your feet facing the Buddha, as this is highly disrespectful. By understanding basic cultural differences I always find that not only do I not offend, but also that showing respect integrates you into a society much more easily.

So this backwards and forwards of outstretched arms goes on for a couple of minutes with differing levels of argument while you try to weave the best price from your vendor.

"I have seven small children and a sick donkey," he tells me.

"I am a poor single girl who loves Indonesia," I try and convince him unsuccessfully.

He comes back with more hard-luck stories and we continue to banter and barter. Finally I throw in the only useful Indonesian I have learnt:

"Bersediakah Anda bersansa dengan saya?"

Which means: "Would you like to dance with me?"!

We laugh a lot at this, have a shimmy together, and finally he says, "For you beautiful lady one thousand five hundred Baht," which is exactly the price I would have paid, and probably exactly the price he wanted in the first place!

After this obligatory bartering with the market trader, I had my precious bundle. That's when the logical side of the brain (absent during the barter process of course) decided to kick in and I had to think how this ball of loveliness was going to fit into my backpack, which to date didn't have enough room for an extra pair of clean knickers, let alone an eight-feet bedspread. The only thing to do was to dispense with redundant items, like extra shoes, socks, a bra and some rather nice toiletries that I had been given as a going-away gift!

Later that month I criss-crossed Indonesia mostly alone in a variety of ways and stayed in a range of accommodation. There was the tranquillity of a small homestay in Ubud where the regular early morning visitor to my porch was a large cockerel I called Steve who, although he had no voice, managed to let me know he had arrived by picking up the banana breakfast left by my host and throwing it against my bedroom door. I was also lucky enough to stay with the Toba Batak people of Northern Sumatra. Their houses are made of wood and are boat shaped, with intricately carved gables and upsweeping roof ridges and are always built with stunning views of the countryside. I stayed in the open plan upstairs room with dramatic views of the valley below. I would sit on the open ledge at the end of the house, forty feet up with my legs swinging and my bedspread wrapped tightly around me, watching a sunset or a sunrise and marvelling at the wonders of Mother Nature and my luck at being able to witness them.

The bedspread proved invaluable everywhere I went and was used as a pillow, a room divider, a picnic blanket and a conversation starter as well as for its planned use as a blanket/bedspread. But the most amazing use was to create a homely feeling during my extended, but not exactly planned, time at Bukit Lawang Orangutan Rehabilitation Centre. I had intended on visiting the area of Gunung Leuser National Park in Northern Sumatra after I had heard about the amazing work being done here. Lover of animals, particular lover of apes and completely besotted by the Orangemen of the Forest as they are known, I was due to spend a couple of days here with the orangutans. I ended up staying and working there for a couple of months: the story of my life, you might be thinking.

The forest in the National Park is dense, humid and in many places impenetrable. There is also a long and undulating river running through it upon which had been built the rehab centre where orangutans are brought. Their journey to this place is one of horror. In many instances, poachers kill female orangutans to get their baby from their still-suckling breast to sell to some rich pathetic individual who thinks it might be 'cute' to have a baby monkey. I wonder if they even know that these animals are great apes. They came to us when they were no longer wanted; could not be controlled or fed; were discarded. They came to us in cages. They needed to remain in ever-larger cages before finally allowing them to go into the forest with older apes, as their terror of freedom was tangible. It was an honour, a delight and an utter privilege to be part of a group trying to save these awe-inspiring creatures.

During my stay in Bukit Lawang (which has now become a well-known eco resort) I had a home. I had a small, wooden, ramshackle shack on the river's edge and when I knew I needed to stay, which was after seeing my first orangutans, I unpacked the backpack completely, something which was and still is rare on my travels. I unpacked and found little hooks in the bamboo construction to place items of clothing, had a special 'hook' for my towel and even the odd memento from my travels. I also unfolded and actually used my bedspread for its original purpose and the difference this one thing made to the room was stunning. There were several other volunteers from different nationalities at the centre. Stuart and Derek were from Manitoba in Canada, Daphne was brought up in Perth and we had three Egyptian sisters who all looked so similar it was hard to tell them apart. My little shack became the go-to place for the other workers and we would take the magic bedspread and snuggle under it together, drinking tea and smoking 'natural' cigarettes supplied by the locals, whilst watching the evening light reveal more Orangemen of the Forest as they played in the low hanging branches of the riverbank trees. I know how to make a home wherever I am and I continued to do so at The Plaine.

*

People do tend to feel very relaxed in The Plaine and upon check-in I always reiterate that *mi casa es su casa* (my house is your house), and please help yourselves to what you need. I love the idea that I have this extended home: yes, it has to be paid for, but you can literally be and do whatever suits you whilst you are here. Many people came to breakfast in their PJs. One lady didn't leave her room for three days, as she was too comfy in the bed. Many children have had to be dragged grumbling out of the door because they 'like it where the crazy lady lives'.

One couple decided that they really, *really* felt at home. They specifically booked the four-poster bedroom for three nights and thoroughly enjoyed their time with us. The only challenge is that this isn't a sprawling hotel with massive insulation and concrete between the floors. It's an old house with rickety floorboards, which create wobbly beds! Noise travels! The first morning after they arrived the couple came downstairs, ate breakfast and went off with a jolly spring in their steps. An hour later my helper Jane came running downstairs. In between bouts of hysterical laughter and snot and tears I got the words, "You... need to... ha ha ha... come and tell me!"

"What, what?" I begged.

"Tell me how to refresh [hospitality term for making it all look lovely for your return] the four-poster room."

I helped this giggling mass upstairs, quite perplexed.

As I opened the door, even I was a little overwhelmed. It wasn't the variety and shape of cords and ties that were strewn about, it wasn't the candlewax and lighters that unnerved me, and it wasn't the fact that all the curtains had been closed round the bed and the slight scent of camphor in the room. It was the gimp mask, the horsehair whip and the pink fluffy handcuffs that sent me into paroxysms of laughter! I have no problem whatsoever with anyone's preferences, but I did find it slightly strange that they would bring them all to a sixteenth-century bed and breakfast in a sleepy Somerset village. We folded where we could and left other things in their exact position. We never did work out what that other leatherette thing was on the chair!

Hans from Sweden also made himself very comfortable in my home and I still blush to think of it. There are rooms on the ground floor and rooms on the first floor. Hans was staying on the first floor. I had checked him in and given him his key with instructions to keep it with him till he checked out.

"May I please leave my key on the hall table when I go to cycle," Hans asked in his lovely Nordic lilt.

He didn't want any extra weight and the possibility of losing the key.

"No problem," I said, and so I presumed that when the key was on the hall table, Hans had left the building. It was with this assumption in my mind that I went to check and refresh his room. Room 4 is at the top of the stairs and it has a small eight-inch step up to the door – which you go up *after* you have opened the door. My mind was a little elsewhere when I popped the key in the door and opened it, because the sight that greeted me sent me almost tumbling backwards. Hans is a little over six-feet tall. He is Swedish (read Adonis) and is very fit (read Adonis again) from all his cycling. Because of his height and the fact that I was eight inches lower than usual, my line of sight was on a level with his nether regions. And the fact that he was standing butt naked in front of me smiling innocently as if this happened all the time made me (and I never thought I would use this word) swoon! He never even grabbed for a towel or anything. Must be something to do with that lovely Nordic open attitude to life. I mumbled, stared, mumbled again and practically fell back off the step and down the stairs. I hid till I heard Hans go out.

Next morning of course, Steph has to make breakfast, despite trying to conjure up a thousand reasons that people should just have toast and a cup of tea that morning. All the other guests had come for breakfast so I had a full house of people, but I was dreading seeing Hans… with his clothes on! Nonchalant – he was nonchalant. He walked in, said good morning to everyone whilst my blush reached my toes and I had to grimace and not make eye contact all through breakfast. I reckon he enjoyed every minute of my discomfort and I think possibly giggled under his breath the whole way through. He definitely gave me an extra-long squeeze when he left!

CHAPTER 20

It's All About Attitude

I hold the firm belief that people are genuinely good and kind and want to help. It has carried me through life and continues to be a mantra that I trust until that trust is broken. Even strangers; even people who turn up to a bed and breakfast with no money to pay their bill and offer to send me a cheque. This happened a few times in the early years of the B&B. We didn't have a credit card machine and only accepted cash or cheques; in 2006 and for a couple of years afterwards it worked perfectly. But still people arrived without the ability to pay. I always took the same stance. Send me a cheque in the mail or transfer the money through your bank. I will never forget Miles's face the first time I offered this option to a departing guest. He was aghast.

"They'll never send the money," he admonished. "There's no way on God's green earth that this person will pay. You must be mad!"

But they did. It happened every time, usually with a lovely note and sometimes with a gift. I knew inherently that they would pay, as to not do so would mean they had to deal with their own conscience and that would be far worse than us going without a payment!

Attitude for me is everything and it means that no matter what is going on and how challenging things might be, you can get through tough times by looking onwards and upwards. And trust me when I tell you that there have been times during the B&B years when having that attitude was an absolute life-saver. We bought The Plaine in 2006 not knowing the first thing really about running a B&B, but having complete faith in ourselves that we could and would do it. And we did. Actually, to be honest, I don't think we had complete faith; I think we just decided to do it and went ahead. No game plan, no due diligence and pretty much no business plan, just a decision to say 'yes' and get on with it. There were massive learning curves along the way, from how to co-ordinate breakfast for twenty when you only own sixteen chairs, to buying in bulk from different suppliers to get the best rates, to providing the tax man, the insurance people and the bank manager with all the right numbers on spreadsheets that looked like hieroglyphics to me. There was also the learning curve that says no matter what your state of mind, health or temperament you must always put your shiny happy face on for the punters, which actually has the dual effect of making you feel happier inside. Have you ever found that you might be feeling a wee bit grumpy or down-in-the-dumps and you see someone smiling at you? So you smile back and all of a sudden your whole demeanour, your mood and your attitude changes. Something so simple can make such a difference and we all have limitless smiles to offer around. Personally, and I know this might sound a little airy-fairy sandal wearer-ish, but it's true, the smile share is the very best thing about any and every day for me, no matter where in the world and how in the world I am doing.

Smiles can also bridge gaps where you didn't think it possible. Thailand has been a great place of adventure for me on several occasions and one particular escapade found me in front of the Commissioner of Police for Bangkok and district. It wasn't anything sinister. I had been in a tuk tuk, the crazy multi-coloured three-wheel hell machines that are part motorbike, part rickshaw and part metal bucket that transport people and their chickens and massive bags of who-knows-what at high speed, perilously throwing the inhabitants around inside. They are like a taxi on speed. And they are always driven by distinctly lean men, never women, who always have on a collared shirt and shorts and flip flops, even though their feet are hanging off the pedals within millimetres of the ground. So, there we were, five of us, relative strangers, heading out to dinner and drinks and dancing so we hopped in the tuk tuk.

These three-wheeled auto-rickshaws are widely used in Bangkok and other Thai cities. The name is onomatopoeic, mimicking the sound of a small engine. We were practically sitting on top of each other, as there is officially only room for three people. Round the corners on two wheels with much hilarity from the passengers, we arrived safely at the Narcissus Club for our evening entertainment. We disembarked with legs and arms flailing and went to pay the nice man who had saved us from death by driving with such dedication.

"I haven't got my wallet," I cried. "My money belt is here and everything else is here but my wallet's gone!"

Luckily the tuk tuk driver was a jolly nice chap.

"I take you back to hotel on same, same road Mrs."

"Yes please," I said and jumped back into the empty tuk tuk away from everyone I knew in Thailand!

We retraced our steps across eight lanes of traffic, round hellishly small lanes and roads in an attempt to find the lost wallet. It was nowhere to be seen, so I needed to get to the police station and Mr Tuk Tuk kindly took me there. Now, for anyone who has not been inside a Thai police station I offer you a word of caution: *don't go*. Most police stations I have seen are grim and soulless and barren of anything even vaguely resembling comfort, but this was a step further than anything I had encountered before: one broken white plastic chair with a crack in the seat that nipped your inner thigh when you sat down, harsh overhead strip lighting with an irregular flicker and the stench of stale urine. It was not somewhere I wanted to be but in order to report my loss and get any compensation from my travel insurance company I knew I needed a police report ASAP after the incident.

"Wait here," the bespectacled, short, perspiring officer said.

Wait is exactly what I did. And wait. And wait. And wait.

Then I went outside to have a ciggie and waited some more.

"Do you have any idea how long it might be till I see someone?" I enquired really, really politely after being there for two hours.

I was told to wait some more as they would be with me "now now", which for those who haven't travelled in Asia means; whenever we get to you but we're really not in too much of a rush. I was parched and tired and a bit fed up, but still I waited. Finally I was led in to see an officer. He had a stark office with an old wooden desk in front of him and a faded picture of a very stern-looking Thai President Prem Tinsulanonda on the wall behind him. But this was no regular officer; this was the Chief of Police, the Commissioner for the area, and he had asked to see me as he was upset that a *farang* (European foreigner) had encountered a bad experience on his watch. He was such a lovely chap and after my initial attitude of weariness and wariness, we chatted away happily. We talked about Thailand and its beauty, its laws on hard drugs and its retribution for law breakers. He regaled me with stories of his time in the UK and then reminded me of the harsh rules surrounding the importation of drugs and the heavy penalties if discovered. Of course none of this was ringing true with me as, crazy as I might be in my adventuring sometimes, hard drugs wouldn't be an option for me, thanks.

However! As we are chatting and smiling and laughing away and he is finally scribbling notes down about the disappearance of my wallet, I start to get a very unnerving niggle about my money belt. It's a thing of beauty, which I have had for years: it has lovely embroidery on the pockets and is perfect for carrying lots of small things. Like the 'small' amount of hashish that my friend Gail had given me so I could enjoy a little smoke later in the evening.

Oh my GOD! I was going to die in a cell in Thailand. I would be disinherited by my family, hated by my friends and defiled by inmates as I wasted away for years in a Thai prison. No more daylight for me, just iron bars and stale urine and food that gave me the squirts. I started to sweat and blush and stammer and tried slowly but surely to edge my way from the office, suggesting to my new police buddy that I really needed to use the bathroom and that I didn't want to waste any more of his valuable time. But he was having none of it.

"I will create you a full police report," he said. "It will be detailed and you can collect it tomorrow morning."

He was diligent and made a complete statement for me. It took ages. He even offered me the name of a person who could translate it into English for my insurance company. Little did he know I was never going to ever set foot into a police station again after making my escape that night. But that wasn't the end of this for me. As if Mr Commissioner knew my dark hashish secret, he decided that as I had been the victim of skulduggery in his country (I don't think I had; I reckon my wallet had just slipped away from me), he needed to make amends and so was determined to take me for a drink to apologise.

"No need," I cried. "I really can just simply go back to my hostel and we can forget about the whole thing," I said politely.

"No, no I insist," he said and gently ushered me, with two fellow officers, into his official car. So by now I had decided that Thai prison wasn't bad enough for me; instead they would put me to work in some weird brothel for men who wanted a tall, white, slightly overweight *farang* to have their wicked way with. Not even the dignity of a jail, just a skanky room and skankier men. They might even dress me up in a little quintessential English dress with Little-Bo-Peep bows and ribbons on it and put my hair in pigtails to enhance the English Rose ensemble. I was paralysed with fear and missed my mum and dad very much right then, but weirdly I still had this inherent belief that all would be well and that if anything happened I would be saved by Colin Firth, as Bridget Jones was saved when her big knickers got her in trouble in the movie. (Obviously I wasn't thinking exactly that as it was only 1985 and the movie hadn't even come out yet, but work with me on this!)

The car rolled on into the Bangkok night and finally after much smiling my way by all three of the inhabitants of the car, we parked and got out in front of what looked like a beautifully posh house with lights glowing and gentle music spilling out. Well, this must be a posh brothel to have all this going on, so maybe they would at least be quite kind to me. We walked in and there were other officers and businessman sitting at low tables. Beautiful diminutive Thai girls dressed in exquisite silk outfits and reeking of femininity served tea and drinks in lovely glasses.

Our group went and sat at a table on lovely soft cushions with bolsters to relax on. I wasn't relaxed. I was wound up like a top.

"Brandy you must have," said Mr Commissioner, as I had endured a rough experience. *Gladly*, I thought, *if this is to be my final evening of freedom before ribbon-wearing hell.* The next thing I know a beautiful Thai girl is proffering me a large brandy and some nibbles (which I declined as squirts are always a potential issue for me in Asia) and my uniformed friends are smiling and raising their glasses to me.

"Could I have a cigarette?" I ask and a light is offered. Momentarily I relax and again my deep-rooted belief that everything would be OK was renewed, but it was sadly short-lived. Mr Commissioner wanted to talk about drugs.

"What do you think about drugs Miss Stephanie? Why do people believe it's OK to bring this hell into my land and to try and export what is grown here?"

Fuelled by a wee bit of brandy, I told him the truth: that I didn't understand, but that there was a huge trafficking of drugs out of Thailand which must also mean that he had his work cut out with internal issues of his countrymen, and not just with *farang*. He agreed, we talked, we laughed and all the time I knew that;

a) I still had my little stash in my pocket and
b) I was surrounded by officers of the law.

Mr Commissioner was the epitome of hospitality and wanted everything to be good for his new friend who was vastly underdressed in her travelling shorts, tie-dyed (of course) shirt and plaited hair in this sea of uniforms and business suits and silk.

Finally he went above and beyond my wildest imaginings.

"Would you like a smoke?" he enquired.

"I have my own cigarettes but thanks for the offer," I smiled back.

He then looked at me knowingly and said, "no-no", a proper smoke. Once again the pictures of the Thai prison cell and its urine stench loomed in front of me and I nearly choked. The Commissioner asked me for a cigarette, gave it to his henchman (well, junior officer probably) and chatted away to me. Not three minutes later Mr Henchman returns with my cigarette and hands it to me but instead of regular tobacco, I can see it's stuffed with hashish. What in the world is a girl supposed to do?

- Option 1. I can smoke it knowing that it's illegal and I am surrounded by feds;
- Option 2. I can drop it on the floor and stamp on it with indignation at the very notion that this upstanding British girl would ever indulge in such a thing;

- Option 3. I can run away screaming into the Bangkok night not having a clue where I am and having no money as my wallet was lost;
- Option 4. I can ask the nice Commissioner if he would like some?

I chose the latter.

He declined.

I seriously didn't have a clue what to do so decided to believe in the intrinsic benevolence of human nature in a man I had never met before, in a land where I was a visitor, in a city I didn't know, surrounded by people who all had a shared history and language, neither of which I understood and to trust a man who held the key to my freedom in his hand. I lit the new cigarette and had a little puff. I then congenially proffered it to the rest of the gang. They all declined. I was stuffed!

As it turns out, and after much extra revelry, some dancing in a very cheesy eighties nightclub and teaching Mr Commissioner some early Michael Jackson moves, hashish is the least of the Thai police's worries and they totally expect us crazy *farangs* to have a little spliff now and then. They aren't so enamoured with the Full Moon parties where drunken stupidness and large amounts of acid and Es drive people nuts and cause havoc, but a little hashish and a little brandy – in their words – never hurt anyone. I didn't end up in the Thai brothel. Instead I had a great night out, met lots of super people, didn't have to wear ribbons or bows or endure urine stench but instead was reminded again that people are usually kind.

*

Over the years this has been reiterated to me but in 2009, it came home to roost with the challenges of the recession that hit the world's economy. It was a particularly difficult year to be in the hospitality business. The costs were the same or more than they were the previous year; the numbers of guests were down due to an uncertain economy; the weather wasn't great and we didn't know how to go about getting more guests through our doors.

But looking on the bright side, the interest rates were lower, which meant more money in our pockets; the weather was actually comparatively nicer than the previous year and the pound was down against the euro, so more people would be looking to spend time in the UK instead of heading abroad! It was an excellent opportunity to galvanise ourselves and set about ensuring we didn't crumble and fold. Instead it was time to recognise this as a period of change and development, of promotion and adjustment and the need to think completely out of the box with great *attitude.*

We looked at our marketing strategy, reviewed our previously pretty much non-existent business plan. We negotiated with suppliers and created new PR avenues by learning more about the illusive intricacies of social media (understood by teenagers and a minefield for anyone else whilst updating brochures and the website. But the most important thing during all of this was our attitude about how it would all work out. And it did. And we were lucky. And I am grateful.

Meeting Mr Commissioner was a remarkable experience as it taught me a valuable lesson in trust. Being able to trust is I think one of the greatest feelings in the world, so even when mine has been tested in both business and personal life, I know that deep down people are good and kind and can be relied upon given the chance.

CHAPTER 21

Ghostly Offerings

I heard the phone ring, then the call of "Coooeee," from the office at the B&B. "Personal call from Wessex Paranormal Society for you, Steph!"

"OK," I replied, actually not giving it too much thought as I was in the middle of counting the millionth pillowcase ready for the laundry collection and wasn't too bothered about who might be on the phone for me personally. So off I went to be greeted by a quite posh and very enthusiastic voice on the other end of the line.

"Hello, yes it's Paul Samson here from the WPS, the Wessex Paranormal Society," he said proudly. He stopped at that point as if I should go 'Arhhh' and 'Ooooh' and 'Wow'. I didn't.

He continued undaunted by my obvious lack of enthusiasm and explained that he and some fellow society members would really appreciate the opportunity to come and investigate my home for spirit activity. Yes I bet you would was my reply, and would they be arriving in a red and white Cadillac wearing full flight suits, have proton particle accelerator packs on their backs shouting 'Where's the ghost?'

When you have a bed and breakfast, you are a sitting target for that quota of your friends who will feel compelled to call you at random and on irregular occasions asking whether you offer rooms by the hour, the rate for a large stag party of over-eaters anonymous or a recommendation for the best room to have a threesome in. All of which must be dealt with in the only way possible which is to go along with their strange fantasies and offer above and beyond what they originally ask for, with the services of gimp masks, bondage and feathers being optional extras, along with a celebratory cake in a style of their choosing. The result of course is that you end up having a giggle with your mates when you have explored all options of various activities, many involving hamsters. It's all good clean fun on the phone followed rather inevitably by a trip to the nearby pub, twenty-seven steps from my front door, to carry on the banter and enjoy a beverage or seven. With this in mind, it was hardly my fault that I wasn't taking this poor man seriously about being from the WPS. But serious he definitely was.

Paul, (fairly normal name), explained to me that he had been a paranormal investigator for many years and had formed the WPS (Wessex Paranormal Society) in 2001. He had a small group of people that he worked with on a regular basis and they would be grateful if we could arrange a time for them to come and visit me and explain what they did, what they would be looking for and how our spirits might show themselves. After a few minutes of me trying to trip this guy up into admitting it was a wind-up, I realised that he was genuine. He really did want to learn more about our spirits and ghosts, and I wasn't going to stand in the way of a man who could tell me more about some of the non-paying inhabitants of The Plaine.

*

I am a believer. In spirits, ghosts or unexplained happenings and occurrences that appear other-worldly. Many people are naysayers and that's their right. I am a believer and enjoy knowing that I have spirits living in my home. They have only ever been unobtrusive, have offered me comfort at times and have never done anything to upset any of the inhabitants of the house. I stand by my belief that they are present and I like the feeling that the past still remains with us.

The term 'haunt' means to visit habitually or appear frequently in the form of a ghost or spirit. My spirits don't do that. They never leave. They simply offer 'proof' of themselves on occasion. Some people believe the ghost or spirit never leaves earth until there is no one left to remember the one who died. Some people are scared of the possibility of ghosts, a fear that is perpetuated through the film industry's portrayal of horror fiction and supernatural happenings. Many cultures and religions believe that the essence of 'being' such as the 'soul' continues to exist after death, whilst many argue that the spirits of those who have died have not passed over and are trapped inside the property where their memories and energy are strong.

There are people who will posit that Einstein proved the existence of ghosts. He maintained that all the energy of the universe is constant and that it can be neither created or destroyed. If this is so, then what happens to our energy when we die? If it can't be destroyed then it must, according to Dr Einstein, be transformed into another form of energy. And this new energy could be called a ghost. Others challenge this by saying that when we die, the energy in our bodies goes where all organisms' energy goes after death: into the environment.

Honestly? I don't care what anyone thinks. I know what I feel and I feel happy and lucky to have made the acquaintance of the spirits in my home. They have always made me feel comfortable even though I might have been wandering alone around a huge sixteenth-century, nine-bedroomed, six-bathroomed, rambling, creaking, higgledy-piggledy house!

And I am not the only one of the family to have experienced the 'feeling' of someone else being around. Ben, the youngest of my super step-children, has had his own array of encounters too. He has often seen movement or felt breath beside him, seen a shadow when no one was around or seen objects move in his room. He is a gentle soul and open to these kinds of things, whereas his twin sister is currently less open and finds the concept threatening. Ben and I didn't mention all the times we knew things had happened… didn't want to freak out his sibling!

Bernice, one of our housekeepers, also saw our spirits. She came downstairs muttering, "That blooming Doctor is getting on my nerves. Why is he always standing in my way?" She had been cleaning Room 2, which is on the first floor and is the only room with a full bathtub. According to Bernice, the Doctor, who wore tweed britches, matching jacket and a dull beige tie, would stand outside the room and, in her words, "grumble about the new-fangled indoor plumbing. 'It'll never work properly, you know'."

He was very clear to her although not to me, but it's interesting that Room 2 was the only room in the house that caused any plumbing problems!

The dining room was a favourite place to have things happen. The key to the cabinet, although firmly placed in the lock, would often be found in the exact corner of the pattern of the carpet, a place too far for it to have been coincidence and too perfect an angle to have been done haphazardly. Chairs would be moved when you turned your back and I often felt someone watching me when I was doing the laundry in the small room off the hall. The spirits that were clear for me were an older gentleman and a middle-aged comfortable brogue-wearing lady. He is the man of the house, the owner and a writer or businessman. He is gentle and genteel. She is the housekeeper. She loves the gentleman deeply and looks after him but can never show her love because, though it is not unrequited, it is unsuitable. Now I know I am a completely hopeless romantic and I do believe in love stories and happy endings so maybe this colours my thoughts, but nevertheless I know what I feel and I know my spirits are real.

*

So I was delighted that the WPS were coming, and we arranged the time and date. I waited with baited breath for the spirit people, the paranormal folk, the (dare I say) Ghostbusters! What to expect? Large burly people in white static suits, big shoes and hats and gloves with a slight smell of disinfectant? Small investigative types with stethoscopes to listen at walls, special lights to illuminate dark crevices and corners or a motley crew of jeans and T-shirt geeks who wanted to look into old homes?

None of the above arrived. Instead we had Paul, Simon and John. Fairly innocuous names and seemingly innocuous fellas, till you dug a little deeper and got to know them a wee bit. Paul seemed 'normal'. In his early thirties, he wore smart jeans and shoes and a collared check shirt. Nothing unusual until he opened his large, black, shiny briefcase to reveal a computer that I am sure could have sent men to the moon and was potentially operated remotely by NASA. It was an all-singing, all-dancing, bells and whistles kind of gadget that made weird and wonderful noises when he tapped the keys. He was very proud that he would be able to create reports and include images through this machine that would support their findings and offer insights into the unexplained movements of The Plaine.

Simon was different. He scuttled into the house and looked around with either nervous or furtive excitement. He reminded me of Penfold the bespectacled hamster (many think he was a mole but I am reliably informed by Google that he was a hamster), who was the reluctant assistant of Danger Mouse in the 1980s series of the same name. He was very keen to show me his gadgets and explain how the EMF detector (Electromagnetic Field Detector) was the modern-day ghost researcher's tracking device, which was used to locate and track energy sources thus detecting fluctuations in the electromagnetic fields. He also had the old-fashioned compass, which would be used in the investigation to indicate spirit presence when the needle cannot come to a precise heading or spins/moves erratically. Finally he had the Spiritcom, which enabled a two-way conversation between the living and the dead. Simon clearly wanted to find ghosts.

Finally, John entered the building, or rather folded himself into the hall. The front door is a regular size door. It's about six feet high and two-and-a-half feet wide but John really had a challenge navigating his bulk through the entrance. I am not suggesting that John is overweight. I am suggesting he is a large fellow and stands at about six feet eight inches in his socks (which by the way I saw as they were all polite and took off their shoes). John explained in his gentle South West of England drawl that he just "looiked sprits and wanned to foind em". I liked John; he had a great smile.

These modern-day Ghostbusters spent a long time in my home over the course of a year. I felt totally comfortable letting them prowl round the property when no one was in and they created a large and in-depth report on their findings. They brought a medium with them at one point and another chap who was so timid I thought he would run away when I spoke to him. They all concurred that yes, there was a lot of spirit activity in the house and yes, there would likely be more activity in the future. Orbs were noted, noises and smells recorded and feelings of movement noted.

I know there are spirits in the Plaine. I never mentioned it on the website or when introducing guests to their rooms but several people over the years have experienced activity of some sort. My favourite was the gentleman who came downstairs one morning with the biggest grin on his face. He had stayed in Room 2 (where incidentally the medium had reported back to me that many people had enjoyed much fun and frivolity over the years, as it was one of the rooms used for fornication when the Plaine was a brothel) and had been woken by someone gently stroking his cheek. This man was a genuine, stalwart no-nonsense Northerner who I am sure would have been a great naysayer had he not experienced this loveliness first hand. He told me with this benign grin on his face, "The hand kept stroking my cheek all through the night so I had the best sleep I have experienced in years."

Spirits, ghosts or energy fields – who cares what people believe in? If something gives them solace, comfort or a nice experience then I am all for it. What matters is that good feelings come when we believe and good feelings should be promoted, I reckon.

CHAPTER 22

Famous and Roman

It's true when I say I have had a variety of famous people sleeping in my bed. It is a fact. And there is no point denying it… I am simply that kinda girl! What that *actually* means is there have been people who are very well known, ergo they are famous and they have stayed in my home. I own the beds in my home therefore they are mine, which means by default that I have had famous people in my bed! When a lovely lady called and booked two rooms, one for her and one for her friend Mr Plant, I did my usual which is to ask the first names of the people arriving. She told me her name was Jane and his name was Rob. Jane wasn't famous or known to me, but could it possibly be that a certain lead singer of one of my favourite bands growing up in the 1980s would be crossing my doorstep? I wouldn't know whether to curtsey, shake his hand or ask if we could headbang together. Led Zeppelin; 'Stairway to Heaven'; OMG! He of course was a totally cool dude who rocked up with snakeskin cowboy boots, a battered old brown leather bag in his hand and wild windswept hair which, when moved out of his eyes, revealed a kind, weathered, brilliant face with an air of mischief all around him. Quiet, unobtrusive and incredibly polite.

"Fancy a drink?" I said.

"Cup of herbal tea would be grand," he replied.

And so, over some ginger and lime infusion we chatted about life, the universe and everything. Then he toddled off to get freshened up before his evening began. Rock 'n' roll lifestyles of the rich and famous, eh? Mr Plant, it turns out, is from the same neck of the woods as me! West Bromwich (famous for having the highest football stadium in England) and Wolverhampton (home of the first set of automated traffic lights in the country), two towns (cities) in the Midlands of the UK from which we sprang. He is an avid Wolves supporter; I was brought up in a household of gold and black (the Wolves colours); he gets what piggie puddin' (pork pie) is and he understands who the two local comedians Aynuk and Ayli are. This particular brand of humour has lots to do with the pronunciation of the Brummy accent and is epitomised by jokes like this:

Posh Lady to boy: "Will your dog bite me if I stroke him?"

Boy: "No Missus."

The lady leans down and strokes the dog, who promptly bites her.

Posh Lady: "I thought you said your dog wouldn't bite me!"

Boy: "This ay mar dog!"

Being from the Midlands means you get lots of flak for having a weird, colourful, sometimes difficult-to-understand accent, but this particular area of the UK has produced a fair few artists who are known not for their inflection but for their music. Slade, UB40, Duran Duran, ELO and the Moody Blues all hail from this area, as does Ozzy Osbourne and the iconic Black Sabbath. So yes, we might speak funny but there is no doubt that there is talent aplenty coming from this much-maligned region, with Mr Plant a shining example… and he stayed in my bed!

*

I have also had Roman centurions in my bed, which is something that I don't think many people can boast about. Many establishments will regale you with stories of ex-kings and queens ('ex' as in they are now dead) and famous politicians and dignitaries having frequented their hostelries, but I don't think many can actually tell you a 'proper' Roman, with his *lorica manica* (armguards) and *paludamentum* (cloak or cape) and a full set of *lorica segmentata* (segmented armour) has stayed in their gaff. I have. In fact I had two fairly high-ranking officials and a sidekick come to stay at the Plaine and they were truly lovely people, and not nearly as smelly as the Roman centurions are reported to have been. Actually they smelled a little like Aramis, that classic symbol of masculinity and sophistication created by Estée Lauder in the 1960s and used by gentlemen 'of a certain age' ever since. I remember giving gift boxes of it to my brothers when I was a young girl. These consisted of a bottle of eau de toilette, some body splash and usually an aftershave. The fact that one of my big brothers (older than me by fifteen years) had sported a beard since I was five seemed to evade both myself and my mother as I wrapped the gift sets each year, and each year my brothers looked benevolently on their little sister and put the boxes to the back of a cupboard for another twelve months. Actually, when I think about it perhaps my mum saved money and just got me to rewrap the same box every year, or is that actually a gargantuan stash of Aramis lurking in the airing cupboard (the depository of many unwanted 'things') in my parents' house?

Anyway, these Romans smelt of Aramis and were awfully polite. They were called John, Jim and Brian and they were in Somerset to visit Roman archaeological sites and explain to groups of visiting school children what it was really like to live in the Roman era. They didn't turn up on my door in regalia, of course. Travelling from Burnley in your Roman attire would have been chafing at best I suspect, so they came in their off-duty gear of jeans and T-shirts. All over six feet tall, which I am reliably informed is tall for a Roman, John was a bookie, Jim a builder and Brian a part-time teacher when they were not being Romans. Their knowledge and enthusiasm for all things Roman was enthralling. We had tea and cake and I listened with interest to some of the stories they would share with the children. Of the Punic Wars of 140 BC, of Caesar and Tiberius and Nero and Claudius, of the forums where politicians spread their word and people sold their wares and, of course, the Gladiators. They explained that whatever subject matter the class 'should' have been studying, it was the gladiators who were the most requested topic of conversation. Their violent confrontations with wild animals, condemned criminals and other gladiators were the main focus of the school children they met. Actually, it turns out that it was the main focus of the *boys* in the schools who were intrigued by bloodshed and combat and knives and having the thumbs-down sign instigated to signal the death of the opponent. Not the girls, just the boys. Hummmmm… interesting.

These Roman improvisers were great company and I knew I had to ask the question: "Would you please come to breakfast in your Roman attire?"

"No problem," they said and I looked forward to the next morning.

Like clockwork, as you would expect from the regimented Romanesque attitude, Jim, John and Brian all came to breakfast on time and in full uniform. Fabulous! Jim, who I felt a little sorry for, was a soldier of menial rank who wore his wool tunic, *braccae* (trousers) and *cingulum militare* (belt) with little or no aplomb or adornment. He would, apparently, have carried his outer gear and armour, but was basically a subordinate to his Centurion buddies. Centurion Brian and Centurion Jim, however, were in full-on regalia and it was splendid. They had lappets, the decorative strips of leather that hung below the skirts; they had red tunics with huge cloaks and huger clasps; there was full-on body armour along with leather leg-wrappings, but to top it all they had the helmets!

The *galea*, originally made of bronze, are magnificent with plumes of dyed red horsehair, sticking up like some crazy Mohican haircuts, and cheek protectors. They are shiny and brilliant and in the dining room at the Plaine with the clunking armour and the sheer size of these guys, it was an impressive sight. I showed them to their table, told them to help themselves to juice and cereal and popped into the kitchen to make coffee for the Romans.

Shortly after the Romans had come in, my other guests arrived to enjoy a hearty start to the day. Jocelyn and Graham were from Kent and were quiet, unassuming and very sweet people who walked in, said good morning to me, obviously clocked the Romans in the corner, but then proceeded to sit at a table not ten feet from the others, eat their breakfast and absolutely avoid eye contact with anyone apart from each other. When they went to the buffet table for cereal and juice they kept their eyes down and shimmied with their backs to the soldiers to avoid any kind of contact. It was as if there were nothing unusual or untoward about having history at the breakfast table, but they definitely weren't going to engage with them. After serving full English to everyone and after a little space for digestion I ambled into the dining room as usual to have a chat. I went to clear Jocelyn and Graham's plates and said quite innocently, "Isn't it interesting to have some Romans eating with us?"

It was light hearted and chatty, but Graham looked at me aghast and said, "Oh my goodness, we didn't even see you there!"

Hummm… Really? It's a big dining room and you may be short sighted but to not have 'noticed' three big burly leather-clad chaps wearing tunics is being even a little too British and reserved for me. After breakfast, the boys packed up and went to have a photo with me outside the front of the house. This happens often when guests leave and it means that my 'just-made-hot-breakfast-in-hot-kitchen-so-a-wee-bit-glowy' face above the necessary pinny will be in all sorts of photos all over the world. The Romans and I were standing on the pavement and it was highly entertaining to watch the faces of passing motorists doing a double or sometimes a triple take. One tractor driver almost knocked over my bollard as he peered at the Centurions from his lofty position atop his John Deere. Most entertaining, though, were the two older ladies who were staying at the George Inn, the pub opposite the Plaine. Dressed in their best crimplene skirts, sensible shoes and with matching perms they were helping each other up the outdoor steps that lead to the Coach Room Suite of the George. Mildred was practically pushing Hilda's portly derriere up the steps when she turned in our direction. The screech was magical. Hilda, in what can only be described as a Souuuuff Lundun accent, cried, "Look over there Mildred, it's a bloody Roman invasion innit?"

They looked over and then collapsed on the stairs in fits of giggles.

"They've got skirts on an' everyfink Hild," said the good lady Mildred.

"'Ere, what you doing in all that get-up then?" they asked our Roman contingent.

And in truly great British spirit, John turned to them and quietly said, "Just roman around Mrs. Just roman around!"

CHAPTER 23

The Journey So Far

There is a famous quote from the American philosopher Ralph Waldo Emerson: 'Life is a journey, not a destination'. I have had quite the journey so far! It has taken me on paths and roads, gravel tracks and railways, up hills and down valleys, and I have walked and crawled and skipped and tripped along them. I have been in and on the water all over this glorious globe and have scuba'd and snorkelled and wondered if the 'nurse' sharks beneath me on the Great Barrier Reef really were as gentle as I had been told. I have been lucky and been in the sky in a variety of different aircraft, some more secure than others.

I was once asked, "Would you like to fly in a microlight over Victoria Falls with me?"

"Yes please," I immediately replied.

I didn't know the pilot, I didn't know his credentials for the mission and I didn't know what condition his aircraft would be in. When I arrived at 6am in the early morning damp mist to meet the pilot of this airborne contraption, I was a little less enthusiastic. It was in fact an ultralight, smaller even than a microlight and even more open to the elements. Picture an egg. A large egg about four feet tall and round with open sides and enough space to just, and I mean just, fit two people sitting next to each other. Now picture a lawnmower engine on the back and a wing above the egg and that's the mechanism in which I will fly over one of the Seven Wonders of the World. Victoria Falls is 1,700 meters in length and reaches over 100 metres drop. Colloquially it is called 'The smoke that thunders' because of its sheer volume and noise. It takes nearly half an hour to get there from a safe take-off point and we travelled above herds of elephant and antelope towards the mist and spray that can be seen from miles around. I wasn't nervous until the flight back.

"Got enough petrol?" I quipped.

"Think so," he shouted over the noise of the little engine.

Whilst flying, I was simply awe-struck and revelling in this journey and the sheer magnitude of the falls. When we finally turned and headed back towards the runway (a plot of flattish grass that is used for take-offs and landings) I looked out and down and saw where we had come from and how close we had got to the edge of the falls and their swirling mist, which I have no doubt would have thermals in it to pull us up and down if the pilot didn't have his wits about him. I hugged him when we landed. I had faith in this man.

*

Most of the things I have done in life weren't really planned and nor was my voyage to the Plaine. I landed there and loved it and bought it and enjoyed it and had most excellent times. By being at the Plaine I learned a lot, but three things are especially profound for me. The first is that I don't need to travel the world to meet engaging, interesting people from different lands. I can meet them in my own country, in my own home and with my own level of hospitality. This won't make me stay in one place forever, but it will make finding a base with a B&B easier in the future. The second is that I love to be able to make a difference. And I did.

Everyday, whether it was through a bit of a giggle, a hug or a good breakfast I made a difference to someone's life and they made a difference to mine. For that I am so very, very grateful. The third thing I learnt is to have faith. I jumped into running The Plaine without due diligence or a business plan. I believed I could create a business that would grow and grow with little or no experience. It was hard going sometimes but I had a firm belief in people and a conviction that things would turn out all right in the end.

As Deborah Moggach wrote in the script for *the Best Exotic Marigold Hotel,* "Everything will be all right in the end, so if it is not all right it is not the end."

My friends and family all knew that no matter how beautiful The Plaine was and no matter what a great business opportunity presented itself, it would not be my destination forever. My journey isn't over. Some people find their destination or their path early on in life. I have a friend who always knew she would be a doctor and she is. Another knew that teaching was his vocation and he has been in the same school educating small minds for twenty-seven years. I don't know what my destination looks like and my journey continues. But what I have learnt is that people are inherently kind. We all have our foibles and idiosyncrasies and our quirks, but fundamentally most human beings are good. I have been lucky to welcome so many people and meet them in their language or mine, and I have greeted the young, the older, the black and the white and people from all corners of the world. We have shared laughter and stories and looked at what makes us different whilst finding what makes us alike. There has been banter and bravado and laughter and love and oodles of fun times on this particular portion of my journey.

I have never been one of those people to wish my life away. OK, so when I was little (and actually even now!) I love Christmas so much that I simply can't wait to see the glee on people's faces when they open their gifts. But I was never one of those people who trudge into work on Monday morning just longing for that Friday 5pm feeling so that they can go home and hide away for the weekend… it's always seemed such a waste to me. I have also never thought of myself as a person who sits with their handbag on their knee and with a slightly knowing Les Dawson-esque look, saying things like 'Ohhhh doesn't time fly?' or 'I just don't know where the time has gone' or that old gem 'It seems like just yesterday that such and such happened'.

And now I have a news flash: *I am that person…* OK, OK, so forget the handbag on the knee and hopefully my face doesn't pucker into the thousand folds that were that great comedian, but replace it with a sneaky G&T and a slightly perplexed look and it's me! I have to admit that I cannot believe that I was in one place for this long. When guests asked how long I had been there, I found myself saying nine years; *Don't be so daft: that would make me *** years old and that can't possibly be true!!!*

But it is true and happily I can report that, although I challenge the passage of time as having been too swift, I can also honestly say that it was an amazing experience and a super few years.

From the Labrador tendencies that Miles and I had towards our first sacrificial guests to the challenges of finding help with the rooms, to the ravages of the exploding drain outside the house, it's been a never-ending source of amazement. There were tears and celebrations and times of wicked humour and genuine compassion.

Sometimes I could have run away.

Sometimes I never wanted to leave.

Sometimes I wanted to work for someone else.

Sometimes I welled up with pride at our achievements.

It's been a rich tapestry and the best bit has always been, and continues to, be the people. We have had everyone from babies to OAPs staying with us, vicars to rock stars, road sweepers and doctors. They have been eccentric and funny, caring and gentle. They have been encouraging, condescending, infuriating and kind. They have stayed a night, a week, a month. They have loved, laughed and relaxed in our home... and we have relished it all!

And it's not just the guests that have stayed with us that have enriched our lives in the past years, but the people of this amazing village too. Never in my wildest dreams could I have imagined a more hospitable, affable, reliable bunch of people, all of whom wanted our business to be a success and cheered us on at every turn. We have the Egg Man who brought our fresh eggs each week, and who then turned out in a howling gale with his chainsaw to help us battle our falling Christmas tree. There was the pub landlord who with his gruff exterior and knowing look saw all and kept his council, but who would in time of need pull out all the stops to help even the newest people in the village. There are people we call friends who genuinely care about us and each other, and have a true sense of community; something so very rare in this mad modern world.

So for those of you who ever thought about going out and buying a B&B and offering your particular brand of hospitality... please try it! Its gruellingly hard work sometimes and you will wonder what on earth you are doing and you will also marvel at the comments people make and the good humour you can share. You will meet all walks of life and all varieties of people so yes... do it... go into B&B land and see what awaits you there!

Ultimately these stories are of what has happened so far. They are a contribution to, not the completion of, my life, my travels and my adventures... oh no! Quite the contrary; there is much more to come. The bricks and mortar of The Plaine weren't enough to hold my heart and body and I still search for new adventures. I guess once bitten by the wanderlust you never quite lose it and so I always look to the horizon to see where is next. What I take from the years there is the ability of kindness to prevail and that we can all make a difference, both in our own lives and in the lives of those around us. I have no idea of my final destination, but I do know for sure that there is a great deal of journeying left in me.

ACKNOWLEDGEMENTS

To anyone and everyone who has been part of this book.

Those who helped create it, those who proof read it…
those who proof read it AGAIN

Those who shared photos.

Those who encouraged me to complete it.

Those who sat me down with wine and didn't let me up till the chapter was finished!

Some for being in it and some for being out of it!

To everyone far and wide who has been part of my fabulous journey so far

A HUGE thank you and please be in touch!!!

www.allaboutsteph.com